CONVERSATIONS AND KEY DEBATES ON INCLUSIVE AND SPECIAL EDUCATION

Based on the second series of the popular *Inclusion Dialogue* podcasts, Joanne Banks explores the tensions, debates and understandings of inclusive education in context of current policy changes. Featuring in-depth interviews with 12 world-renown academics, this book provides a comprehensive overview of the current tensions and conceptual understandings in the field.

Delving further into diverse viewpoints around special education, and how mainstream education includes and excludes students, Banks broadens the discussions started in the first podcast series by highlighting nuanced alternative perspectives, national contexts and historical developments. Given the diversity of the authors themselves in terms of their geography, career stage and views on inclusive education, the chapters highlight key issues around how we theorise inclusive education, the diversity of views on how inclusion can be measured and the intersections between disability and other student characteristics such as socio-economic background, gender, ethnicity, race and sexuality. Using the informal interviews as its springboard, the book offers practical insights into universally designed pedagogies and the role of the school community in fostering inclusive education.

This book is ideal for academics, researchers and educators working in inclusive and special education, who wish to create more inclusive environments for their students. It is also a key resource for policymakers seeking to understand inclusive education and address its manifestation in learning environments on ground.

Joanne Banks is a lecturer and researcher in Inclusive Education at the School of Education, Trinity College Dublin. She has previously published *The Inclusion Dialogue* (2023, Routledge).

CONVERSATIONS AND KEY DEBATES ON INCLUSIVE AND SPECIAL EDUCATION

Global Insights from 'The Inclusion Dialogue'

Joanne Banks

Routledge
Taylor & Francis Group
LONDON AND NEW YORK

Designed cover image: © Martin Dean

First published 2025
by Routledge
4 Park Square, Milton Park, Abingdon, Oxon OX14 4RN

and by Routledge
605 Third Avenue, New York, NY 10158

Routledge is an imprint of the Taylor & Francis Group, an informa business

© 2025 Joanne Banks

The right of Joanne Banks to be identified as author of this work has been asserted in accordance with sections 77 and 78 of the Copyright, Designs and Patents Act 1988.

With the exception of Chapter 5, no part of this book may be reprinted or reproduced or utilised in any form or by any electronic, mechanical, or other means, now known or hereafter invented, including photocopying and recording, or in any information storage or retrieval system, without permission in writing from the publishers.

Chapter 5 of this book is freely available as a downloadable Open Access PDF at www.taylorfrancis.com under a Creative Commons Attribution (CC-BY) 4.0 license.

Any third party material in this book is not included in the OA Creative Commons license, unless indicated otherwise in a credit line to the material. Please direct any permissions enquiries to the original rightsholder.

Open access funding provided by Linnaeus University.

Trademark notice: Product or corporate names may be trademarks or registered trademarks, and are used only for identification and explanation without intent to infringe.

British Library Cataloguing-in-Publication Data
A catalogue record for this book is available from the British Library

ISBN: 9781032705415 (hbk)
ISBN: 9781032711331 (pbk)
ISBN: 9781032705484 (ebk)

DOI: 10.4324/9781032705484

Typeset in Times New Roman
by KnowledgeWorks Global Ltd.

This book is dedicated to Dermot Farrell who continually reminds us to think inclusively in everything we do.

ACKNOWLEDGMENT

Though he is no longer with us, we remember James Kauffman with gratitude and respect.

CONTENTS

Acknowledgment	*vi*
List of Figure and Table	*ix*
About the Editor	*x*
Contributor Bios	*xi*
Foreword	*xv*

Introduction: Diving deeper into international debates in inclusive education 1
Joanne Banks

1 Mainstreaming the concept of equity and inclusion into Bangladeshi education: What can we learn from the experience? 7
Mohammad Tariq Ahsan

2 Looking back, looking forward: Progressing inclusive education 23
Suzanne Carrington

3 A personal reflection across decades of education 32
Chris Forlin

4 What "all" means 45
James M. Kauffman

5	Theorising the inclusionary–exclusionary continuum while investigating school situations *Johan Malmqvist*	62
6	Contemporary complexities of inclusive education in the United States *Amanda Miller and Susan Gabel*	76
7	Inclusion: Musings on process *Srikala Naraian*	86
8	Learning from others: Comparing institutionalizations of special and inclusive education *Justin J.W. Powell*	96
9	Are we preparing teachers to include or exclude? *Umesh Sharma*	109
10	Reinventing the square wheel: The past and future of special and alternative education *Sally Tomlinson*	119
11	Crossing disciplinary boundaries in inclusive education *Joanne Banks*	129

Index *136*

FIGURE AND TABLE

Figure
5.1 The Staircase Model of Inclusionary and Exclusionary Processes.   65

Table
1.1 Mainstreaming equity and inclusion in the National Curriculum 2022 in Bangladesh   15

ABOUT THE EDITOR

Joanne Banks is a lecturer and researcher in inclusive education at the School of Education in Trinity College Dublin. Joanne's research interests are in the field of inclusive education and educational inequality. She has published widely on special and inclusive education policy and practice, school exclusion and student diversity. She is the presenter and author of the Inclusion Dialogue podcast series' and books.

CONTRIBUTOR BIOS

Tariq Ahsan, University of Dhaka, Bangladesh

Professor Dr. Mohammad Tariq Ahsan has been working at the Institute of Education and Research (IER) of the University of Dhaka since 2001. His specialisation areas are Educational Change and Pedagogical Reform, Equity and Inclusion in education and Teacher preparation. Tariq has vast experience for the development of National Frameworks/standards in the areas of specifically focusing on National Curriculum Framework Development, equity and inclusion, SDG 4, Global Citizenship Education (GCED), ECCD, Education in Emergency for Geographically Displaced Children and Adolescent Skill Development. Tariq conducted a significant number of research studies on education and published more than 100 papers in the forms of national and international journal articles, books, conference proceedings, periodicals and reports. His research manuscripts were published in high-impact prestigious journals like the *Oxford Encyclopedia* and *Cambridge Journal of Education*. Tariq is the founding editor of an international journal titled *Asian Journal of Inclusive Education* and reviewed many research papers for several prestigious journals. Tariq was involved in the editorial process of many publications and been keynote speakers at international conferences. As an honour of Tariq's contributions at the country and regional levels, he received several international awards.

Suzanne Carrington, Queensland University of Technology

Suzanne is a Research Professor in the Centre for Inclusive Education QUT Australia. She has over 27 years of experience working in universities including teaching, research, international development and various leadership roles. Her areas of expertise are in inclusive education, ethical and transformative leadership for inclusive schools, disability and teacher preparation for inclusive schools. She has engaged in research with industry collaboration to inform policy and practice in Australian and international education contexts. With her research colleagues, she has received over 4 million dollars in research funding. She has published over

100 journal publications, books, book chapters and research reports. She is currently the Program Director of the School Years Program for The Cooperative Research Centre for Living with Autism (Autism CRC). http://www.autismcrc.com.au/

Chris Forlin, University of Notre Dame, Australia

Professor Chris Forlin is a Research Fellow at the University of Notre Dame Australia. She is also an international education consultant specialising in supporting governments and school systems to implement effective and quality inclusive education. She has worked in the field of education for more than 40 years as a teacher, university lecturer and government advisor. Her extant research and publications focus on policy development for education reform and systemic support for children and youth with disabilities; and the development of inclusive curriculum and pedagogy with a particular emphasis on inclusion in developing countries. Her most recent book, published by Emerald (2022), is on transition programs for children and youth with diverse needs published in the International Perspectives on Inclusive Education series that she edits.

Susan Gabel, Wayne State University, United States

Dr. Gabel (she, her, hers) was a public school special education teacher for 15 years, during which she taught in Michigan and Kentucky. Her school teaching experience spans the full continuum of special education support services, including segregated facilities, self-contained classrooms in regular schools, resource rooms, and full inclusion. Dr. Gabel's largest body of scholarly work is situated within disability studies in education, broadly examining the institution (e.g., education) as a site of exclusion of difference, particularly as it produces disability-as-difference. Using a social interpretation of disability, Dr. Gabel has examined the ways institutional structures produce disability. Therefore, disabled people are not the focus. Rather, the focus is on disability as it is produced by ableism. More recently, Dr. Gabel has used feminist affect theories to illustrate some consequences of ableism. Via this approach she explores the materialism of emotions produced by ableism. Most recently, Dr. Gabel reflects on a career of inclusion activism and has more questions than answers about inclusion, leaving her contemplating the implications of her scholarship and activism. In 2021 and 2022 she directed the NEH Summer Institute for Teachers, Disability and identity in history, literature and media.

James M. Kauffman (1940–2024), University of Virginia, United States

James M. Kauffman was Professor Emeritus of Education, the University of Virginia, where he joined the faculty in 1970. His Ed.D. (1969) was from the University of Kansas, and in 2011, he received the distinguished alumni award from the University of Kansas School of Education. He was a past president of the Council for Children with Behavioral Disorders and a former teacher of both general elementary students and special education for students with emotional and behavioural disorders. He was author or co-author and editor or co-editor of more than 30 books, many book chapters and many journal articles. Garry Hornby and he edited a special issue of Education Sciences, which published as a book in 2021 and titled

Special and Inclusive Education: Perspectives, Challenges and Prospects. In 2020, he edited a volume titled "On educational inclusion: Meanings, history, issues and international perspectives"; he was also editor of the book, *Revitalizing Special Education: Revolution, Devolution, and Evolution* (2022).

Johan Malmqvist, Linnaeus University, Sweden

Johan is a Professor in the Department of Pedagogy and Learning at Linnaeus University. Johan, together with Disa Bergnehr and Linda Fälth, leads the research environment Research in Inclusion, Democracy and Equity (RIDE) https://lnu.se/forskning/sok-forskning/research-in-inclusion-democracy-and-equity-ride/ . Johan's research is primarily oriented towards the area of special needs education and special education. It focuses on issues related to inclusion-exclusion and equity. More specifically, Johan is engaged in developing knowledge about schools' and other educational organisations' capacity to meet learner's various prerequisites and needs. Other research interests are within theory development and methodology.

Amanda Miller, Wayne State University, United States

Amanda L. Miller (she/her) is an assistant professor and critical educator in the Division of Teacher Education at Wayne State University in Detroit, Michigan. Her research is framed by humanising approaches to inquiry, critical theories (e.g., disability critical race theory, critical spatial theory) and qualitative and visual methods, including photovoice and cartography. Her research focuses on how school systems, policies and practices impact girls of colour, including girls who identify with or have been labelled with disabilities, as well as how they create joy and care in schools. She also works with educators to create classroom and school communities that are culturally responsive, culturally sustaining, and inclusive and families to generate equitable and just family-school-community partnerships. Amanda has recently authored/co-authored publications in *Disability & Society*, *International Journal of Inclusive Education*, *International Journal of Qualitative Studies in Education* and *Teachers College Record*. In 2020, she was awarded the Outstanding Dissertation Award from the AERA Disability Studies in Education SIG and the Dissertation of the Year Award from the University of Kansas School of Education.

Srikala Naraian, Columbia University, United States

Srikala Naraian is a Professor of Education in the Department of Curriculum and Teaching at Teachers College, Columbia University. She locates herself in the disability studies tradition and is interested in qualitative inquiry in inclusive education and teacher preparation for inclusive education. Alongside her research in US public schools, Dr. Naraian has also prepared teachers for inclusive education in international contexts; she has served as a Fulbright Specialist in Germany and in India. She has published widely in many journals including the *International Journal of Inclusive Education*, *Teachers College Record* and *Curriculum Inquiry*. Her recent books include *Narratives of Inclusive Teaching: Stories of Becoming in the Field* (2021), co-authored with Sarah Schlessinger, and *Teaching for Inclusion: Eight Principles for Equitable and Effective Practice* (2017).

Justin J.W. Powell, University of Luxembourg

Justin J.W. Powell is Professor of Sociology of Education in the Institute of Education & Society at the University of Luxembourg. His comparative institutional analyses chart persistence and change in special and inclusive education, in vocational training and higher education and in science systems and research policy. His research—bridging sociology, political science and education—has been widely published in English and German and received numerous international awards. After coordinating international dissertation fellowship programs at the Social Science Research Council (SSRC), New York, he was Research Fellow of the Max Planck Institute for Human Development, Berlin; Lecturer at the University of Göttingen; T.H. Marshall Fellow at the LSE; and Project Director at the Social Science Research Center Berlin (WZB). In Winter 2011/2012, he was Visiting Professor of Sociology at Leibniz University Hannover, Germany. He was Research Fellow of the Institute of Higher Education Research of the Martin Luther University of Halle-Wittenberg, Germany (2012–2016) and Visiting Research Fellow at the University of Oxford, UK (MT 2020).

Umesh Sharma, Monash University, Australia

Umesh Sharma is a Professor in the Faculty of Education at Monash University, Australia and the Associate Dean (Equity and Inclusion). Umesh's research programs in areas of disability and inclusive education span India, Pakistan, China, Bangladesh, Fiji, Solomon Islands, Vanuatu and Samoa as well as Australia, Canada, the USA and New Zealand. He is the chief co-editor of the *Australasian Journal of Special Education* and the *Oxford Encyclopedia of Inclusive and Special Education*. He has authored over 175 academic articles, book chapters and edited books on various aspects of inclusive education. His co-authored book *A Guide to Promoting a Positive Classroom Environment* received the International Book Prize Award from the Exceptionality Education International. He was named the top Special Education Researcher in Australia (2019) based on his work's impact locally and internationally by the Australian Chief Scientist. More recently, he was identified as the 'most prolific author' in the field of inclusive teacher education (ITE) and inclusive education respectively based on systematic bibliometric reviews examining the work of highly cited inclusive education researchers in the last 25 years. His main areas of research are positive behaviour support, inclusive education for disadvantaged children and policy and practice in special and inclusive education.

Sally Tomlinson, Goldsmiths London University, England

Sally Tomlinson is Emeritus Professor at Goldsmiths London University and an Honorary Research Fellow in the Department of Education, University of Oxford. She has spent nearly 40 years teaching, research and writing about special and inclusive education, the politics of education, and race, ethnicity and education. Her most recent books are *A Sociology of Special and Inclusive Education*' (Routledge 2017) and *Education and Race from Empire to Brexit* (Policy Press 2019). She is currently writing a book on 'Ignorance' (Agenda Press).

FOREWORD

There have been recent rapid changes internationally in inclusive education policy and practice. The pace of innovation offers immense opportunities to learn from practice in other systems and how they may, or may not, help inform local developments. However, the pace of change is itself a challenge, with the length of the peer-reviewed publication process meaning that recent policy developments and current debates are not often well captured in the academic literature. This book fills this gap, using insights from highly regarded international scholars from a broad range of countries to provide accessible and up-to-date information on debates and developments internationally.

The book provides crucial information not only for academics and students but also for policymakers by providing insights into developments in very different educational systems. In reflecting on such insights, it is important that we do not engage in policy borrowing, suggesting that aspects of one system can be simply 'imported' into another regardless of the societal context. Rather, we need to engage in policy learning, that is, looking at how specific policies operate in the broader societal and political context of a particular system. From this perspective, comparative research can shed light on particular policy levers that may or may not work in different settings and on the unintended consequences of particular interventions. The contributions in this book point to a number of potential levers for securing progress in inclusion.

A further contribution of this book is its foundation in a process of dialogue. Dialogue between researchers often takes place at conferences and academic meetings, out of sight of the public and policy community. Based on a second series of podcasts, and building on a previous edited collection, this book shows the value of documenting discourse around inclusive education. It is particularly valuable that many of the contributors share their own life stories and what prompted them to conduct research on and advocate for inclusive education. Joanne Banks's warm but probing interaction style in her interviews with international scholars makes the reader feel they are listening in to the best of current debates and prompts us to reflect on our own assumptions and perspectives.

Emer Smyth
Economic and Social Research Institute, Dublin

INTRODUCTION

Diving deeper into international debates in inclusive education

Joanne Banks

Introduction

When we focus on issues related to inclusive education, the conversations can quickly veer into themes that go far beyond our education system. The way education systems and schools respond to student diversity is often at the heart of social, economic and political thinking about difference and otherness. Since the publication of the first Inclusion Dialogue book, *The Inclusion Dialogue: Debating issues, challenges and tensions with global experts*, and Series 1 of the Inclusion Dialogue podcast, the debate about whether to provide special or segregated forms of provision for students with disabilities or offer fully inclusive systems seems somewhat less polarised. The open and frank discussions in this first book provided nuances to many of these opposing arguments offering greater understanding of the complexity of defining inclusion in different contexts, highlighting the anomalies in national and international policy and exploring the role of inclusive pedagogy and frameworks to overcome barriers to education to children and young people. The use of two modes, audio through the podcast and the written word, through the book, has generated interest and engagement among student teachers, teachers and school leaders wishing to create more inclusive school environments for students. The engagement from the policy community is perhaps most notable however suggesting a major gap between academic thinking and empirical research those involved in policy decision making. By making this rich academic work accessible, this series of podcasts and books offers a way to bridge the gap between theory and practice.

This volume builds upon these foundational discussions in the first book by diving deeper into some of the issues raised. In Series 2 of the Inclusion Dialogue podcast, I spoke with leading academics from around the world to continue these rich

2 Conversations and Key Debates on Inclusive and Special Education

conversations and explore new ideas, systems and practices. This book includes contributions on special and inclusive education in Bangladesh, Australia, India, the United States, Sweden, the United Kingdom and Belgium with many of the authors bringing comparative research perspectives to the discussions. The role of history in shaping current thinking and provision features heavily in many of the chapters who describe the social, cultural, economic and often political factors shaping the evolution of special and inclusive education over time. Geography is also evident in the book chapters as we learn of special and inclusive education in different social contexts in the Global North and South whilst also gaining insights into countries and contexts where the authors have undertaken empirical research throughout their careers. This book takes an holistic view of inclusive education, and many of the discussions note the intersections of social class, culture, ethnicity, gender and disability. These conversations take place against the backdrop of disciplinary and theoretical structures, such as disability studies and the sociology of (special) education which, some of the contributors argue, can guide and facilitate ongoing discussions around system and curriculum reform as well as school and classroom level practices.

Academic podcasting

This book differs from other academic books in that it exists in tandem with a podcast available in audio and video. While academic podcasting has grown in popularity in recent years as a way to communicate academic research, ideas and thinking, this book provides an alternative and complementary mode of communication. A notable feature of podcasting in recent years is the way in which they can be produced with little technical expertise and administrative oversight (Cox et al., 2023) allowing academics to create and produce their own content. This mode of communication cuts through much of the time-lag associated with much academic work. For academics producing this kind of scholarship, it allows for the production of knowledge without mediators or gatekeepers from more traditional academic outputs such as books and journal articles. In doing so, however, debates about its use have tended to focus on whether it counts as scholarly communication (Cook, 2023a, 2023b).

Aside from these debates, however, is the ability of a podcast to democratise knowledge reach new audiences. Across many disciplines, podcasting is offering a way in which to bring academic work into mainstream conversations and distil complex ideas and understandings (Kinkaid et al., 2020). This liberation of knowledge changes the relationship between the listener and the text with some commentators suggesting that the debates that arise from the podcasts can be more valuable than the podcast itself (Conroy & Fletcher-Saxon, 2024).

The Inclusion Dialogue podcast was originally created to improve student engagement in academic work and there is a growing recognition of academic podcasting as a valuable method of teaching and an effective way in which to reach students and nurture teacher-student relations (Conroy & Kidd, 2023). Cook (2023a) describes the opportunities within podcasting as a 'novel teaching and learning format' (p. 3) that offers a way for listeners to be critical and self-reflexive (SpokenWeb Archive of the Present, 2021). In doing so, this medium has the opportunity to change how the audience or listenership responds to information allowing them to explore the challenges and nuances present in any academic work.

An unintended consequence of podcasting, and this is certainly true in the case of Inclusion Dialogue, is how they enable more inclusive collaborations across communities of researchers and allow for the 'breaking down' of boundaries between different cultural and geographical contexts. This community building goes further, in the extent to which podcasts can connect people from within and outside academia and allow for the extension of ideas and engagements between stakeholders allowing us to 'bypass the institutional lock-in experienced by other traditional formats' (Cox et al., 2023, p. 2). The nature of audio and the use of voice in this way humanises the researchers thus broadening communities of stakeholders and allowing the opportunity to include partners or stakeholders not traditionally engaged in academic work. In education, this can often mean those involved in policymaking but also educators, school leaders, support staff, parents and students.

The contributors

Each chapter of this book is authored by a podcast contributor who used the transcript of the interview as the basis of their work. The focus of the chapters varies widely in accordance with the areas of expertise of the individual authors but several central themes form the basis of most of the contributions giving some insights into the context of policy decisions around special and inclusive education and others describing how inclusion can be implemented and the barriers to implementation. Given the diversity of the authors themselves in terms of their geography, career stage and, most importantly, their views on inclusive education, the chapters highlight key issues around language, context and culture, policy and rights in how we discuss this critical topic. Many of the chapters are written through an interview approach that consists of excerpts from podcasts where interviewees share their personal motivations and critical turning points in their professional careers working in inclusive and special education settings. Other chapters build on the podcast conversations highlighting relevant theories and providing relevant empirical research to support these discussions. Both of the approaches taken to the chapters in this book offer the opportunity for readers to deepen their awareness, reflect on their own perspectives and recognise the complexity of inclusive education as a subject area.

This section provides a brief overview of key themes raised in the chapters of this book:

Tariq Ahsan is a Professor at the Institute of Education and Research (IER) of the University of Dhaka in Bangladesh. His chapter provides a critical review of inclusive education policy, strategy and implementation over time highlighting the difference in the discourse around inclusion between Asian countries and other Western contexts. Professor Ahsan discusses the recent transformation of education in Bangladesh based on curricular reform which he argues are underpinned by principles of equity and inclusion in education. He details how these changes have sought to promote flexible, community-focused experiential learning using continuous formative assessment to increase access and participation.

Suzanne Carrington is a Research Professor in the Centre for Inclusive Education, Queensland University of Technology (QUT) in Australia. Using her early career experiences, this chapter provides a rich understanding of what has shaped Professor Carrington's research and scholarship throughout her career. In particular, she draws into focus some of the critical factors in the implementation of any inclusive system of education emphasising two critical stakeholders: parents and school leaders. The chapter examines the role of parents, and the school community more generally, in changing mindsets and creating equity for every student. Professor Carrington also emphasises the role of transformative school leadership in developing inclusive systems and gives insights into her recent research on supporting leaders to create and sustain equitable and inclusive schools.

Chris Forlin is a Research Fellow at the University of Notre Dame Australia and an international education consultant specialising in supporting governments and school systems to implement effective and quality inclusive education. In this interview and chapter, Professor Forlin provides a rich understanding of the development of special and inclusive education across the different national contexts that she has worked in throughout her career. The chapter highlights key moments from her early career that have motivated her research and shaped her academic thinking. She discusses the importance of quality teacher education in any implementation of inclusive practices in schools and highlights the need for schools to be able to easily measure inclusion and have frameworks for implementation. The chapter closes with her recent research in the Philippines post-COVID and the impact of teaching in Volatile, Uncertain, Complex, Ambiguous (VUCA) contexts on inclusive education.

Amanda Miller and Susan Gabel are from the Division of Teacher Education at Wayne State University, Detroit in Michigan in the United States. This podcast discussion and chapter highlight the complexities of the special and inclusive education debate in the United States. They discuss the change and development of theory, policy and practices that are focussed on disability bringing attention to what they describe as 'deficit laden remnants' persist and reproduce. The chapter draws on their recent research on girls of colour with complex support needs and a study of youth-led and family-centred solutions in inclusive education.

James Kauffman (1944–2024) was the Professor Emeritus of Education, the University of Virginia, and past president of the Council for Children with Behavioral Disorders and a former teacher of both general elementary students and special education for students with emotional and behavioural disorders. James' Chapter provides a much needed counter position to the majority of chapters in this book. In essence, he questions the 'all means all' movement and argues that instruction that is appropriate for the student is more important than placement in mainstream education. He differentiates between inclusive education and instruction on the basis of disability which he believes cannot be readily compared with other forms of diversity among students.

Johan Malmqvist is a Professor in the Department of Pedagogy and Learning at Linnaeus University, Sweden. Johan, together with Disa Bergnehr, leads the research environment Research in Inclusion, Democracy and Equity (RIDE) https://lnu.se/forskning/sok-forskning/research-in-inclusion-democracy-and-equity-ride/. The podcast discussion and chapter provide a rich understanding of special and inclusive education in Sweden now and over time. Malmqvist draws our attention to increases in special education diagnosis with a particular focus on student behaviour and social order in Swedish schools. He raises concerns around trends in disability diagnosis and student segregation which is attributes to political decisions that are not underpinned by pedagogical empirical research.

Justin Powell is Professor of Sociology of Education in the Institute of Education & Society at the University of Luxembourg. This chapter explores the role of comparative research in inclusive education and highlights how these approaches can be crucial in addressing theoretical, methodological and practical challenges and concerns. Using examples from Powell's research in North America and Europe, he uses a multi-disciplinary approach to explore the tensions in defining inclusion in different national contexts and discusses the anomalies in many systems that continue to categorise students with disabilities and, often, have expanded segregated provision 'under the banner of inclusion'. His focus goes beyond education to the critical transitions for students as they progress from compulsory education to further education or employment.

Srikala Naraian is a Professor of Education in the Department of Curriculum and Teaching at Teachers College, Columbia University. This chapter provides a fascinating discussion on the epistemological lenses we can use working in the area of inclusive education. Naraian describes the influences of her own teaching background on her research and scholarship before exploring the role of disability studies in present-day debates on inclusion and student diversity. She questions the application of universal understandings of inclusion and stresses the need to view inclusion as a process that is continually in motion.

Umesh Sharma is a Professor in the Faculty of Education at Monash University, Australia, where he is the Associate Dean (Equity and Inclusion) with research programs in the area of disability and inclusive education spanning India, Pakistan, China, Bangladesh, Fiji, Solomon Islands, Vanuatu and Samoa as well as Australia, Canada, the USA and New Zealand. This interview and chapter give a rich insight into Sharma's early career and the factors that have influenced his academic research and thinking. The chapter explores, however, the critical role of teacher education programmes in inclusive education focussing on the Global South. He describes an 'overemphasis on theory, misconceptions about inclusion, colonial influences and a lack of exposure to inclusive practices' and proposes the use of five key principles to reform inclusive teacher education and create inclusive schooling systems across different education systems in the Global South and North.

Sally Tomlinson is an Emeritus Professor at Goldsmiths London University and an Honorary Research Fellow in the Department of Education, the University of Oxford with forty years of teaching, research and writing about special and inclusive education, the politics of education, and race, ethnicity and education. In Sally's interview and chapter, she describes both her career and the development of special and inclusive education in the United Kingdom. Using the sociology of special education perspective, she highlights the intersection of poverty, race and special education over time. The chapter discusses key tensions in the inclusive education debate today in the UK focussing on the 'government attempts to fix a broken system' by creating a parallel form of alternative provision 'despite an ideology of inclusion'.

References

Conroy, D., & Fletcher-Saxon, J. (2024). What are educational podcasts? https://www.bera.ac.uk/blog/what-are-educational-podcasts

Conroy, D., & Kidd, W. (2023). Using podcasts to cultivate learner–teacher rapport in higher education settings. *Innovations in Education and Teaching International*, *60*(6), 861–871. https://doi.org/10.1080/14703297.2022.2102528

Cook, I. (2023a). *The future of scholarly podcasting can still be whatever we want it to be*. https://blogs.lse.ac.uk/impactofsocialsciences/2023/06/14/the-future-of-scholarly-podcasting-can-still-be-whatever-we-want-it-to-be/

Cook, I. (2023b). *Scholarly podcasting: Why? What? How?* Routledge.

Cox, M., Harrison, H. L., Partelow, S., Curtis, S., Elser, S. R., Hammond Wagner, C., Hobbins, R., Barnes, C., Campbell, L., Cappelatti, L., De Sousa, E., Fowler, J., Larson, E., Libertson, F., Lobo, R., Loring, P., Matsler, M., Merrie, A., Moody, E., & Whittaker, B. (2023). How academic podcasting can change academia and its relationship with society: A conversation and guide [perspective]. *Frontiers in Communication*, *8*. https://doi.org/10.3389/fcomm.2023.1090112

Kinkaid, E., Emard, K., & Senanayake, N. (2020). The podcast-as-method?: Critical reflections on using podcasts to produce geographic knowledge. *Geographical Review*, *110*(1–2), 78–91. https://doi.org/10.1111/gere.12354

SpokenWeb Archive of the Present (2021). *Podcasting as a Field of Critical Study*. https://www.youtube.com/watch?v=lyI6NdGIORc

1
MAINSTREAMING THE CONCEPT OF EQUITY AND INCLUSION INTO BANGLADESHI EDUCATION

What can we learn from the experience?

Mohammad Tariq Ahsan

Introduction

Since the Salamanca Declaration in 1994 (UNESCO, 1994), countries around the world have made significant efforts for ensuring equity and inclusion in education. However, it is evident from the global reform towards equitable and inclusive quality education that the notion of equity and inclusion has raised various conceptual confusions and malpractices that led to even exclusions in the name of inclusion (Slee, 2010). Exclusions took place, in most cases, while education systems in different countries attempted to include children with disabilities in the mainstream settings. In line with that, the UN Convention on the Right of Persons with Disability in 2006 (UN Enable, 2008) has further rearticulated the issue of "Disability inclusion" from the human rights perspective that aims to have access to quality services, acceptance and participation of persons with disabilities within the services. Despite global initiatives, countries in different geographic regions experienced challenges in implementing inclusion in different aspects of social structures. A review of UNESCO (Kaplan & Lewis, 2012) in the Asia Pacific region reported that many countries in this region introduced segregated initiatives such as ensuring access of children with disabilities as per labelling their conditions (i.e. mild, moderate, severe) and designing separate training for teachers for orienting equity and inclusion in education. The report further claimed that many countries established separate monitoring systems/cells in the education system for ensuring equity and inclusion. Some countries introduced separate teaching-learning and assessment strategies for children with disabilities. As a result, mainstreaming the notion of equity and inclusion in education remains an illusion for many countries. Therefore, country- and context-specific narratives are required to understand the concept of equity and inclusion in education for identifying implementation strategies for making the notion happen (UNICEF, 2020).

It is evident from extensive research in Asian countries (Forlin, 2008, 2010; Singal, 2010; Singal & Muthukrishna, 2014) that equitable inclusive educational experiences

DOI: 10.4324/9781032705484-2

are much different than from the Western contexts (Croser, 2004; Miles, 1997; Mittler, 2000) because of numerous socio-cultural and demographic factors. Ahsan and Malak (2020) conducted a review on teachers' teaching efficacy for inclusive practices in several Asian countries published in the Oxford Research Encyclopedia of Education. This review paper indicated that class size, gender context, content and length of teacher education programme, level of teaching involved, and familiarity with the relevant persons and the specific country contexts significantly contributed to conceptualising and implementing varied forms of equity and inclusion in education.

Bangladesh, like many other countries in the world, has taken a wide range of policy and strategic initiatives for ensuring equity and inclusion in mainstream education since the early 1990s. Being one of the densely populated developing countries situated in South Asia, Bangladesh has many contextual and regional factors that need deeper exploration to understand the journey towards equity and inclusion in education in Bangladesh. Currently, Bangladesh is going through a large-scale educational transformation, where it is claimed that the issue of equity and inclusion is embedded throughout the process that may have the potential to make inclusion a mainstream concept. Through the analysis of evidence and author's personal experiences for over twenty-four years, this paper presents the journey towards educational transformation in Bangladesh for making the system equitable and inclusive for all. The journey towards educational reform for ensuring equity and inclusion in education could be divided into two time periods.

i Pre-Bangladesh period
ii Bangladesh period

(i) Pre-Bangladesh period: Historically, the education system in primitive (3000 BC to 1600 AD) Bangla (known as Pathshala, Toll, Maktab) was community based and flexible in nature. In that model of education, teachers designed the curriculum based on the aptitude and ability as per the student diversity, parental demand and the demands of socio-economic and geographical characteristics of local contexts. Therefore, the curriculum was co-designed by teachers, students, parents and local stakeholders. Pedagogical approaches were mostly personalised and experiential, and the assessment system followed was formative. There was no centrally controlled structured curriculum. In the early 1900, the colonial industrial model of public education commenced in this region. Mostly behaviourist model (Fosnot, 1996; Steffe & Gale, 1995) of curricular and pedagogical approaches was followed around the world, and the Greater Indian education system was no different from the global practice. Hence, the colonial industrial model of public education introduced centrally controlled, teacher-focused, memorisation-based, examination oriented and market-driven education. Later in 1947, after 200 years of colonial regime, Grater India was divided into two countries: India and Pakistan and a part of Bangla was declared as East Pakistan. During the Pakistani period until 1970, the West Pakistani dominated and followed almost the Colonial Industrial model.

Access and participation of mass people in education immediately before the pre-Bangladesh period were not satisfactory. Asadullah (2010) reported that dropout rate in East Pakistan was 68.25%, gross enrolment rate in primary education was around 45%, and the retention rate after two years was 23.25%. This status reflects the overall equity and inclusion status in education of East Pakistan period.

(ii) Bangladesh period: In 1971, Bangladesh got independence through a liberation war. One of the major objectives of our war of independence was to ensure equity and social justice to eradicate inequality in every aspect of life including education. For developing an inclusive society through an accessible education system for all, the Constitution of the People's Republic of Bangladesh strongly stated articulated:

Article 17: "establishing a uniform, mass oriented and universal system of education and extending free and compulsory education to all children to such stage as may be determined by law" (Ministry of Law Justice and Parliamentary Affairs [MoLJPA], 2000, p. 5).

Article 28: "No citizen shall, on grounds only of religion, race, caste, sex or place of birth be subjected to any disability, liability, restriction or condition with regard to access any place of public entertainment or resort, or admission to any educational institution'" (MoLJPA, 2000, p. 8).

In line with the strong constitutional declaration, the first education commission of the independent Bangladesh known as the Kudrat-E-Khuda Education Commission Report 1974 proposed a flexible, equitable, inclusive and student-centred curricular approaches for the newly independent Country. Therefore, it can be claimed that the policy reform for equity and inclusion started in the early 1970s in Bangladesh. After being a signatory of the Education for ALL-EFA in 9990 (UNESCO, 1990), Bangladesh enacted the Compulsory Primary Education Act 1990 (MoPME, 1990) for ensuring free and compulsory education for all children. Specifically, parental awareness and responsibilities were articulated, and financial penalties were introduced for not sending their children to school. In contrast, Section 27.3.3 (e) of the Act states "The decision of a primary education officer [can be] that is not desirable to enter a child in a primary institute on accounts of being mentally retarded" (MoPME, 1990). Due to such statement, segregation of children with disabilities was generally perceived as legally alright by the stakeholders.

In line with the EFA initiatives, the National Education Policy (NEP) 2010 was also enacted as a comprehensive framework for future education reform. The NEP 2010 proposed several educational reform activities including gender and inclusion in education. The NEP 2010 mentioned the education for diverse learners within its main objectives (MoE, 2010, pp. 1–2). Besides, inclusive education was formally recognised by the policy as a strategy for achieving quality education. Although the NEP 2010 has recognised the educational rights of children with disabilities, it may spark debate among advocates for these children because the policy does not explicitly mention "inclusion" or "inclusive education". A critical analysis of the policy reveals that many of its statements are broad and often vague in their intent (Malak, 2014). While the policy contains various sections that emphasise education for all children, it does not explicitly state whether children with disabilities will attend the same schools as their nondisabled peers. For instance, Section 18 (7) notes, "Separate schools will be established according to special needs and in view of the differential nature of disabilities of the challenged children" (MoE, 2010, p. 43). Consequently, such approaches were found to be segregated initiatives for education of children with disabilities (Ahsan & Burnip, 2007; Ahsan & Mullick, 2013).

Several policies have been enacted in Bangladesh specifically focusing on children and persons with disabilities. The first national policy on disability known as "National Policy for the Disabled" developed in 1995 mentioned about special, integrated and inclusive educational opportunities as the educational right for children with disabilities. This policy was considered as the drafting of the first legislation on persons with disabilities in Bangladesh titled "Bangladesh Disability Welfare Act 2001". The Act clarified the definition of disability, as well as their right to education, health, safety, employment, accessibility, social security and more. The third section of the Act ensured that opportunities must be created in mainstream education for children with disabilities (MoSW, 2001). However, the Act defined the concept of disability from the medical model perspective and being considered as a barrier to ensuring equity and inclusion education, as this labelled children with disabilities from the deficit or medical model perspectives and considered disability-related activities from the welfare perspective (Šiska & Habib, 2013). Consequently, the 2001 Act was revised and the new Act known as the "Rights and Protection of Persons with Disabilities Act, 2013" was passed in Parliament for removing the limitations of the previous Act. One significant contribution of this Act is that it clearly mentioned that children with disabilities must not be forbidden from enroling in mainstream educational settings (MoSW, 2013). However, some statements of the Act contrast with the concept of equity and inclusion in education.

It is noticeable from the critical analysis that despite favourable features several limitations were identified in every policy reform initiative (Ahsan, 2013; Ahsan et al., 2012, 2015; Malak et al., 2014; UNESCO, 2018) that might act as contradictory to the concept of equity and inclusion in education. Such contradictions must have an impact on the educational practices for equity and inclusion in education.

Reflection of educational policy reforms into practice: What does evidence reveal?

Inclusion happens when favourable policies are rightly translated to the operational strategies and then implemented with appropriate understanding and skills in the field. Inclusion initiatives in education first officially took place by the Ministry of Primary and Mass Education of the government through the Primary Education

Development Programme Phase 2 (PEDP II) at the primary level and the Teaching Quality Improvement (TQI) project under the Ministry of Education at the secondary level education in Bangladesh (Ahsan & Burnip, 2007; Ahsan & Mullick, 2013). Critical review of the operational document of the PEDP II (DPE, 2003) indicates that the conceptual understanding of the inclusion in education provided for a holistic approach to the inclusion and full participation of all learners which it stresses cannot be achieved by simply continuing to make schools available and continuing with the same practices which already exclude some children from school. The concept of inclusion in education (IE) was seen as:

> an approach to improve the education system by limiting and removing barriers to learning and acknowledging individual children's needs and potential. The goal is to make a significant impact on the educational opportunities of
>
> 1 Those who attend school but who for different reasons do not achieve adequately, and
> 2 Those who are not attending school but who could attend if families, communities, schools and the education system were more responsive to their requirements.
>
> *(DPE, 2003)*

However, the implementation strategies of the IE described in the same document could not translate the concept, rather promoted segregations. For example,

- a separate cell on IE was established for implementing IE in Education. As a result, different divisions of the Ministry did not own the IE initiatives as their regular responsibility. Consequently, separate human resource development, monitoring mechanism initiated instead of embedding the concept into the mainstream initiatives,
- instructions for the inclusion of children with disabilities promoted medical/deficit models as teachers were asked to label children with disabilities as mild/moderate/severe/profound and only mild and moderate children with disabilities were allowed to be enroled in the schools,
- special education experts inserted special education components in the teacher education curriculums for making those inclusive,
- instead of implementing IE as a holistic approach to ensuring every learner's learning through addressing individual needs and potential and removing barriers to learning, the IE approach in PEDP II identified four target groups that included gender, special needs/disability, tribal community and vulnerable children. Hence, separate strategies and action plans were developed for addressing targetter interventions.

(Ahsan & Burnip, 2007; Ahsan & Mullick, 2013;
DPE, 2011a, 2011b, 2011c, 2018)

Such confusing start of IE implementation is now surprising as the review of Kaplan and Lewis (2012) of IE practices in the Asia Pacific region found that labelling, screening by non-technical persons, target group-oriented segregated interventions, inserting special education into the existing curriculum existed in the strategic documents and in practice. One possible reason at that beginning stage could be that there was not enough model/practice or evidence regarding how to implement IE was not available to the experts and practitioners. Therefore, they tried to scratch ideas from the segregated models like special education approaches. In line with that, the evaluation of PEDP II conducted by Jacqui Mattingly (2010) noted,

> The move towards greater inclusion and equity must be seen as a continual process of development which builds on what is already in place. Rather than seeing inclusive education as a separate activity it must be adopted and integrated into all aspects of the programme and be reflected in all programme activities. This means all Prog 3 activities will need to be routinely examined and reported through an 'inclusive lens'. The Access and Inclusive Education Cell will need to work collaboratively to promote inclusion and support and monitor activities across line divisions and other institutions to ensure the system moves towards inclusion for all. The re-establishment of focal points in each line division in DPE would therefore be beneficial to ensure this collaboration and the integration of inclusive issues in all aspects of the programme.
>
> *(p. 13)*

It was expected that learning through the evaluation of PEDP II would help to design a more comprehensive programme during PEDP III and IV. But it seemed that PEDP III and IV were designed in a way to continue the PEDP II actions again without any major changes (ACIE, 2017). On the other hand, in secondary education, after completion of TQI project, the IE initiatives did not exist due to not mainstreaming the idea of inclusion. Though there was a progressive definition of IE, Bangladesh conceptualised and implemented it differently. Misconceptions, dissimilarities, partial understanding and inconsistency between the concept and the implementation are being observed around the globe. Many contradictory concepts and practices while implementing inclusive education. Hence, such initiatives hindered the achievement of the broader goal of equity and inclusion for ensuring quality education for all. It was vital to recognise that IE was not just a matter related to those with special educational needs but an issue for all children. Consequently, the IE initiatives remained as segregated approach that only implemented some targeted interventions.

Despite initiating various interventions for ensuring equity and inclusion in education since 2003, Bangladesh was facing several equity-related challenges in relation to educational access, active participation, achievement and acceptance. For example,

- Bangladesh Bureau of Educational Information and Statistics (BANBEIS, 2022) report on students' access and participation in 2022 revealed that overall 71% of the total student population of Grade I are dropped out from the system from different layers. This includes 14%, 35.66% and 21.14% dropouts at primary (Grade I–V), secondary (Grade VI–X) and higher secondary (Grade XI and XII) levels, respectively.
- the recent National Student Assessment (NSA) in 2002 (MoPME, 2022) found that over 50% of the learners do not achieve competencies in language and communication and two-third of the students do not achieve competencies in numeracy. This 71% of our student population represents those who have socio-economic challenges and special educational needs. They mostly find the education system very rigid to address their needs and consequently drop out. Interestingly, these large number of dropped out population enter the job market as unskilled and illiterate manpower and paid less as a result.
- Bangladesh Bureau of Statistics (BBS, 2023) report indicates that around 2.5 million jobless youths currently exist in Bangladesh who completed schooling. Among them, 8 hundred thousand have university degrees even. Besides, female participation in the job market is not yet satisfactory.
- As per the Intellectual Property Statistical Country Profile 2022 Index, Bangladesh's patent application position is 93rd (WIPO, 2023). This is another indication that despite having approximately 170 million population, the current education is not contributing to develop a knowledge-based economy.
- Despite declaring primary education compulsory and free, the Campaign for Popular Education (CAMPE, 2014) study reported that a huge urban-rural and economic inequity existed due to practicing memorisation-based summative assessment systems. Such assessment approach led the whole education system to promote coaching and guidebook business and made education expensive.
- Due to not reflecting the concept of equity and inclusion correctly in the operational strategies and practices, pre-service teachers (Ahsan et al., 2012, 2013), in-service teachers (Ahmmed et al., 2014; Islam & Ahsan, 2022) and institutional heads (Ahsan et al., 2011, 2012) possess a mixed and confused understanding of equity and inclusion. In some cases, they conceptualised IE as an additional task that required additional resources and time allocation.
- Studies (Ahsan et al., 2012, 2013) further found that Bangladeshi female teachers possess positive attitudes but have less teaching efficacy for including all learners in mainstream education. Besides, they are yet reluctant to include children who have high support needs (Ahsan & Sharma, 2018).

Facing such challenges for long period in education, the National Curriculum and Textbook Board (NCTB) under the Ministry of Education (MoE) conducted several studies to identify the challenges of the existing education system and also rigorously reviewed the global trends of the educational change. Besides, several contemporary research studies were also done. Specifically, two separate studies were conducted by NCTB based on the reviews of the contemporary pre-primary and primary education curriculum (NCTB, 2019a) and on secondary curriculum (NCTB, 2019b). Findings of those studies show that curriculum development initiatives for pre-primary, primary, secondary and higher secondary levels were done separately, which hampered the consistency of the learning continuum in different education layers. The studies further found that the contemporary curriculums were very much centrally controlled, rigid, memorisation-based and teacher-centric. In addition, the assessment systems did not focus on formative feedback to learners, only paper-pencil-based, content memorisation-focused summative assessments were followed. These practices resulted in forcing learners to fit into the system's demands instead of making system learner friendly.

The NCTB studies (NCTB, 2019a, 2019b) further found that the learning objectives and competencies in the contemporary curriculums were articulated focusing on contents and ignored the values and attitudes part in most cases. The articulation of competencies was close-ended and did not promote multiple ways of expression (i.e. students will be able to verbally explain….). Based on the review of global trends of educational reform, the studies also reported that globally there is a demand for educational transformation to come out of the traditional approach of curriculum due to fulfilling the necessity of fourth industrial revolution, mitigating challenges like COVID-19 emergency situations, and having the benefits of the demographic dividend that Bangladesh is currently going through. Critical analyses of the findings of the studies revealed that such traditional approaches are hindering the students' access, active participation, learning achievements and acceptance of learners resulting in high dropout rates. Hence, the studies recommended a need for curricular transformation. In view of this, a new initiative was taken to develop a seamless curriculum from pre-primary to grade XII, which aim to infuse learners with high values and enable them to adapt to new realities of the coming future and survive in competitive world conditions by acquiring competencies and upholding self-identity through nurturing individual needs and potentials. Studies recommended to develop a future transformative competency-based curriculum by introducing experiential pedagogy, formative assessment, making system decentralised, contextual and flexible so that the curriculum can address individual and contextual needs for ensuring quality education by achieving equity and inclusion. Based on the research findings, review of global practices and conducting series of consultation with the stakeholders, the "National Curriculum Framework-2021" (NCTB, 2022b) has been developed, which aims to bring the transformations to mainstream the notion of equity and inclusion in education.

Educational transformation for mainstreaming equity and inclusion since 2021

The National Curriculum Framework 2021 (NCF, 2021) was the first policy document in Bangladesh that aimed to design a seamless curriculum for from pre-primary to Grade XII. The NCF 2021 philosophically promotes the values of "Equitable" view instead of "Deficit" of equity and Inclusion (NCTB, 2022b) that clearly articulates that the target group for ensuring equity and inclusion in education are all children who are in and out of education. Further to this, the NCF 2021 mentioned that Universal Design for Learning (UDL) would be the principle to be followed in the pedagogical and assessment approaches. In addition, NCF 2021 further claimed that a gender transformative approach to be embedded for breaking the gender stereotypes of the society as mentioned in the NCF 2021 (NCTB, 2022b). All these approaches were embedded in the curricular initiatives of the National Curriculum 2022 for all learners as a mainstream approach. Specific gender and inclusion instructions were also mentioned in the detailed curriculum and assessment strategy documents for ensuring individual needs and potentials (NCTB, 2022a, 2023a). Table 1.1 provides some practical examples of how equity and inclusion were mainstreamed in the National curriculum 2022.

TABLE 1.1 Mainstreaming equity and inclusion in the National Curriculum 2022 in Bangladesh

Topic	Challenges in contemporary approach	New curricular approach
Competency articulation	Most competencies and learning outcomes were content-focused and close-ended that did not promote multiple ways of expression of students' achievements (i.e. students will be able to verbally explain different parts of a tree). Such competency articulation promoted memorisation and did not give students freedom to express their learning. Consequently, children who could not verbally explain the topic were excluded.	Students' performance focused that attempted to capture the combined abilities of a learner's knowledge, skills, attitudes and values. Multiple ways of expressions were maintained (i.e. students will be able to express the importance of plants and functions of their structure for nourishing them in everyday life for making environment sustainable). Learners gain knowledge, skills, attitudes and values collectively and they have freedom to choose the ways of expressing their understanding and skill as per their need and abilities (i.e. written, diagram, picture, photo, gesture, sign, song, etc.).

(*Continued*)

TABLE 1.1 (Continued)

Topic	Challenges in contemporary approach	New curricular approach
Subject dimension	No defined subject dimension was present that could conceptualise the strands of that specific transdisciplinary relationship. Hence, subject-based equity and inclusion issues were also not considered. In Language and communication subjects (Mother Tongue Bangla and Foreign Language English) previously competencies were on four skills based only that include reading, writing, listening and speaking. It had three challenges: a language was mechanically learnt instead of acquisition process due to segregated skill development approach b content-focused and memorisation-based language learning approach missed the speaking, critical writing skills c Children who have physical, sensory or intellectual challenges could not meet the competencies ever as the overall communication model was missing.	Subject dimensions were clearly defined for all ten learning areas. All subject dimensions covered human diversity, equity and inclusion notions as a cross-cutting notion. In Language and communication subjects (Bangla and English) overall communication model was captured in the subject dimension. Hence, students were given experience of language acquisition by exploring the surrounding environment and expressing their thoughts and learning through four skills as well as through other alternative approaches. Consequently, learners could achieve all four skills, express in multiple ways that contributed in nourishing learners' individual needs, potentials and creativity. Such an approach ensured equity and inclusion of all learners in language acquisition. As Language and communication are the vehicle for learning other subject dimensions, this approach was embedded in other subjects for exploring learning environment through five senses and expressing those in multiple ways. Please see the diagrams of two languages and communication as reference of ensuring equity and inclusion that was presented in the NCF 2021.
Pedagogical approaches	Teacher-centred, content-focused, lecture-based and memorisation-focused. Individual performance and competition in a group were the key to such pedagogical approach.	Experiential learning pedagogical approaches (Kolb, 1984) were applied that provided learners opportunity with exploring concepts from multiple sources, internalise those through cooperative learning strategies (Johnson & Johnson, 2013) and then express learning in multiple ways. Such flexible pedagogical approaches assisted all learners to nourish their individuality, creativity,

(*Continued*)

TABLE 1.1 (Continued)

Topic	Challenges in contemporary approach	New curricular approach
		alternative expression abilities and grow up as a community. Besides, group work and pair work provided all students opportunity with get support from each other. Hence, separate instruction to support a child with disability to someone next to that student became redundant.
Assessment strategies	Memorisation-based summative paper-pencil tests were applied. Such a process created a rigid and time-bound assessment process that put students in a stressful environment. Hence, students who cannot cope with these rules and regulations do not pass and are excluded. Only assessment of learning was considered. Extra time allocated only for students with disabilities. A stenographer is allocated for students with visual impairment. Penalty is given to the students if any writing error occurs due to stenographer's fault.	Formative pedagogical approaches have been followed to ensure assessment. It offered a flexible model of assessment that gave a whole school day for learners to participate in the assessment process, learners could express their learning in multiple ways, along with performance indicators teachers could also assess learners' behavioural indicators that assisted to capture the holistic development of a learner. Moreover, such assessment ensured assessment for learning, as learning and of learning as a part of learning journey. Such flexible learning assessment opportunity promoted equity and inclusion for ensuring active participation of all learners in the assessment process.
Learning materials	Textbooks were the mostly used learning material	Textbooks became resource books that connected learners with multiple sources for information collection. As a result, textbooks, complimentary books, online sources, surrounding environment, places, and human beings everything turned into learning materials. This provided opportunity with all learners exploring learning materials as per their interest, ability, context, requirements. This also opened the use of multi-sensory learning materials for all. Such opportunity is very supportive to ensure equity and inclusion,

(*Continued*)

TABLE 1.1 (Continued)

Topic	Challenges in contemporary approach	New curricular approach
Learning environment	Students with disabilities were labelled and segregated in the classroom by rigid learning environment. For example, students with disabilities were asked to sit in the front row. A friend sitting next to children with disabilities was asked to support the child with disabilities.	Learning environment went beyond classroom. School compound, home, community people and places were connected in the experiential learning cycle. It assisted learners who live in home for some reasons, continue learning even in any COVID-19-like emergency, also support from parents or any teaching assistant became a mainstream regular practice for ensuring individual learning needs.
Gender transformative approach	Separate chapters were written for conceptualising gender issues.	Gender transformative ideas have been embedded in the whole curricular approaches in multiple ways. For example; a In Bangladesh, doing housekeeping, cleaning, caregiving and cooking activities are considered mostly as the responsibility of a female family member. To break such gender stereotypes, examples of roles are distributed across the subjects and in diagrams of the textbooks. b In the Life and livelihood subject, all students were asked to practice housekeeping, cleaning, caregiving and cooking at home and in educational institutions. This led the learners; family members and community members to experience a new gender role around their regular environment. Some reactions were initially observed due to a shake in their beliefs that were considered as the symptoms of the process of breaking the gender stereotype in the community. c In Bangladesh, games are also divided according to gender types. In the Wellbeing subjects, all games were introduced for all students. In the History and Social Science subject, the female Football team was introduced as a part of the exploring plurality of identity among us.

(*Continued*)

TABLE 1.1 (Continued)

Topic	Challenges in contemporary approach	New curricular approach
		d Despite having higher female participation in primary education in Bangladesh, secondary education completion rate and participation in the job market are very poor among females. Hence, the Life and livelihood subject introduced different occupation courses compulsory for all learners. e Third gender as a part of human diversity and gender as a crosscutting issue in different subjects and illustrations were also maintained.

Conclusion: What research reflect about the educational transformation in Bangladesh?

A ten-year (2017–2027) long phase-wise implementation plan has been designed for the educational transformation in Bangladesh. Several studies have been done till to date on the experiences and effects of curricular transformation in Bangladesh. Firstly, a piloting study (NCTB, 2022a) was done in 62 educational institutions across various geographical locations in Grade VI before implementation of the new curriculum across the country. In addition, some operational studies (NCTB, 2023b; UNICEF & CIPRB, 2023) were also done while the new curriculum was implemented in Grades VI and VII nationwide.

Stakeholders' engagement is an important indicator of the success of any educational transformation. According to the piloting study, students' active participation and collaboration increased significantly. In piloting institutions, 87.79% of the students demonstrated full active participation and around 11.68% of the students exhibited partial active participation in session activities. Moreover, students' motivation to learn things increased significantly that contributed in higher attendance rates of the learners. Parent participation in learning activities remained a bit passive as approximately 60.63% of parents fully participated in session activities. However, considering the previous approach, such participation was satisfactory. Approximately 97% of the teachers have a fully comprehensive understanding of TG. But some teachers expressed their concerns and disbelief about the new curricular approach as around half of the teachers asked for more training on new approaches. Such concerns were also found in parental attitudes through qualitative interviews. Specifically, their major concern was the shift of the assessment process from a quantitative model to a qualitative approach. However, the operational studies (NCTB, 2023b; UNICEF & CIPRB, 2023) found improving trends in the overall situation. Some resistance from urban-based schoolteachers and parents was observed, which was also noticed in India, Estonia and Canada during the transformation journey. Challenges still remain in teacher education, teacher status, monitoring and mentoring mechanisms that need to be aligned with the curricular transformation in Bangladesh. Overall, the experience of embedding the notion of equity and inclusion into mainstream educational transformation approach brought a positive reflection on access, active participation, learning achievements and acceptance of diverse learners in the education system. Bangladesh is yet to expand the transformation journey in Grades X, XI and XII by the year 2027. Learning of this transformation journey could raise some thought-provoking issues for further academic debate around the globe.

References

Ahmmed, M., Sharma, U., & Deppeler, J. M. (2014). Variables affecting teachers' intentions to include students with disabilities in regular primary school in Bangladesh. *Disability and Society, 29*(2), 317–331.

Ahsan, M. T. (2013). *National baseline study for 'developing a model of inclusive primary education in Bangladesh project' based on secondary data.* Plan Bangladesh.

Ahsan, M. T. et al. (2015). *Situational analysis of education of children with disabilities in Bangladesh.* Sightsavers.

Ahsan, M. T., & Burnip, L. (2007). Inclusive education in Bangladesh. *Australasian Journal of Special Education (AJSE), 31*(1), 61–71. https://doi.org/10.1080/10300110701255807

Ahsan, M. T., Deppeler, J., & Sharma, U. (2013). Predicting pre-service teachers' preparedness for inclusive education: Bangladeshi pre-service teachers' attitudes and perceived teaching-efficacy for inclusive education. *Cambridge Journal of Education, 43*(4), 517–535. https://doi.org/10.1080/0305764X.2013.834036

Ahsan, M. T., & Malak, M. S. (2020). Teaching efficacy and inclusive practices in Asian countries. *Oxford Research Encyclopedia of Education.* https://doi.org/10.1093/acrefore/9780190264093.013.1227

Ahsan, M. T., & Mullick, J. (2013). The journey towards inclusive education in Bangladesh: Lessons learned. *Prospects, 43*(2), 151–164. https://doi.org/10.1007/s11125-013-9270-1

Ahsan, M. T., & Sharma, U. (2018). Pre-service teachers' attitudes towards inclusion of students with high support needs in regular classrooms in Bangladesh. *British Journal of Special Education, 45*(1), 81–97. https://doi.org/10.1111/1467-8578.12211

Ahsan, M. T., Sharma, U., & Deppeler, J. (2011). Beliefs of pre-service teacher education institutional heads about inclusive education in Bangladesh. *Bangladesh Education Journal, 10*(1), 9–29.

Ahsan, M. T., Sharma, U., & Deppeler, J. M. (2012). Exploring pre-service teachers' perceived teaching-efficacy, attitudes and concerns about inclusive education in Bangladesh. *International Journal of Whole Schooling, 8*(2), 1–20.

Ahsan, M. T., Sharma, U., & Deppeler, J. (2012). Challenges to prepare pre-service teachers for inclusive education in Bangladesh: Beliefs of higher educational institutional heads. *Asia Pacific Journal of Education (APJE), 32*(2), 1–17. https://doi.org/10.1080/02188791.2012.655372

Asadullah, N. (2010). Educational disparity in East and West Pakistan, 1947-71: Was East Pakistan discriminated against? *The Bangladesh Development Studies, XXXIII*(3), 1–46.

Asian Centre for Inclusive Education-ACIE (2017). Making education system inclusive through PEDP4: What does it mean? *Presentation on inclusive education working group seminar.* ACIE.

BANBEIS (2022). *Bangladesh education statistics 2021*. BANBEIS.

Bangladesh Bureau of Statistics- BBS (2023). *Quarterly labour force survey 2023*. BBS.

CAMPE (2014). Whither grade V examination? An assessment of primary education. *Completion examination in Bangladesh*. CAMPE.

Croser, R. (2004). *Supporting students using assistive technology in an inclusive education framework*. Retrieved March 14, 2011, from www.arata.org.au/arataconf04/papers/doc/croser.doc

DPE (2003). *Seconf primary education development programme (PEDP2): Programme document*. DPE.

DPE (2011a). *Third primary education development programme (PEDP3): Main document*. DPE.

DPE (2011b). *Third primary education development programme (PEDP3): Implementation guide*. DPE.

DPE (2011c). *Third primary education development programme (PEDP3). Annexes*. DPE.

DPE (2018). *Fourth primary education development programme (PEDP4): Programme document*. DPE.

Forlin, C. (2008). Education reform for inclusion in the Asia-Pacific region: What about teacher education. In C. Forlin & M.-G. J. Lian (Eds.), *Reform, inclusion and teacher education*. Routledge Tailor and Francis.

Forlin, C. (2010). Reforming teacher education for inclusion. In C. Forlin (Ed.), *Teacher education for inclusion: Changing paradigms and innovative approaches*. Routledge Taylor & Francis.

Fosnot, C. T. (1996). *Constructivism: Theory, perspectives and practice*. Teachers College Press.

Islam, T., & Ahsan, M. T. (2022). Attitudes of English medium school teachers in Bangladesh towards inclusive education: Challenges and possible solutions. *International Journal of Whole Schooling*, *18*(2), 54–87.

Johnson, D. W., & Johnson, R. T. (2013). The impact of cooperative, competitive, and individualistic learning environments on achievement. In J. Hattie & E. Anderman (Eds.), *International handbook of student achievement* (pp. 372–374). Routledge.

Kaplan, I., & Lewis, I. (2012). *Promoting inclusive teacher education*. UNESCO.

Kolb, D. A. (1984). *Experiential learning: Experience as the source of learning and development* (Vol. 1). Prentice-Hall.

Malak, M. S. (2014). Special education today in Bangladesh. In A. F. Rotatori, J. P. Bakken, F. E. Obiakor, S. Burkhardt, & U. Sharma (Eds.), *Special education international perspectives: Practices across the globe. Advances in special education* (Vol. 28, pp. 585–622). Emerald Group Publishing Limited.

Malak, M. S., Begum, H. A., Habib, M. A., Banu, M. S., & Roshid, M. M. (2014). Inclusive education in Bangladesh: Are the guiding principles aligned with successful practices? In H. Zhang, P. W. K. Chan, & C. Boyle (Eds.), *Equity in education: Fairness and inclusion* (pp. 107–124). Sense Publishers.

Mattingly, J. (2010). *Impact evaluation study of second primary education development programme*. IMED, DPE.

Miles, M. (1997). Disabled learners in South Asia: Lessons from the past for educational exporters. *International Journal of Disability, Development and Education*, *44*(2), 97–104.

Ministry of Education (2010). *The national education policy*. Ministry of Education. Retrieved from http://www.moedu.gov.bd/index.php?option=com_content&task=view&id=338&Itemid=416

Ministry of Law Justice and Parliamentary Affairs (MoLJPA) (2000). The constitution of Bangladesh revised. Government Press. Retrieved from http://bdlaws.minlaw.gov.bd/act-367.html

Ministry of Social Welfare (2001). *Bangladesh persons with disability welfare act*. Retrieved from https://legislativediv.portal.gov.bd/sites/default/files/files/legislativediv.portal.gov.bd/page/64379df1_f98c_47ff_b9e6_cbcabadd8ece/26.The%20Rights%20and%20Protection%20of%20Persons%20with%20Disabilities%20Act%2C%202013.pdf

Ministry of Social Welfare (2013). *Rights and protection of persons with disabilities Act-2013*. MoSW.

Mittler, P. (2000). *Working towards inclusive education social contexts*. David Fulton Publishers.

MoPME (1990). *The compulsory primary education act 1990*. MoPME.MoPME. 2022.

MOPME (1990). *The compulsory primary education act, 1990*. Dhaka: MOPME.

NCF (2021). *National Curriculum Framework 2021*. Bangladesh: National Curriculum and Textbook Board.

National Curriculum & Textbook Board (2022a) *Study report on curriculum piloting in grade 6*. NCTB.

National Curriculum & Textbook Board (2023a) *Exploring the effectiveness of new textbooks at secondary grade six and seven in Bangladesh*. NCTB.

National Curriculum & Textbook Board (2023b) *Rapid assessment impact study, Bangladesh*. NCTB.

National Curriculum & Textbook Board- NCTB (2019a). *Situation analysis of secondary curriculum in Bangladesh*. NCTB.

National Curriculum & Textbook Board-NCTB (2019b). *Effectiveness, situation analysis and needs assessment of current pre primary and primary curriculum of Bangladesh: A compilation of key findings*. NCTB.

National Curriculum and Textbook Board (2022b). *National curriculum framework 2021: Pre-primary to grade 12*. NCTB.

Singal, N. (2010). Doing disability research in a Southern context: Challenges and possibilities. *Disability & Society*, 25(4), 415–426.

Singal, N., & Muthukrishna, N. (2014). Introduction: Education, childhood and disability in countries of the South – Re-positioning the debates. *Childhood*, 21, 1–15.

Šiska, J., & Habib, A. (2013). Attitudes towards disability and inclusion in Bangladesh: From theory to practice. *International Journal of Inclusive Education*, 17, https://doi.org/10.1080/13603116.2011.651820

Slee, R. (2010). Political economy, inclusive education and teacher education. In C. Forlin (Ed.), *Teacher education for inclusion. Changing paradigms and innovative approaches*. Routledge.

Steffe, L. P., & Gale, J. (Eds.). (1995). *Constructivism in education*. Lawrence Erlbaum Associates.

UN Enable (2008). *Convention on rights of persons with disabilities*. Retrieved September 17, 2010, from *http://www.un.org/esa/socdev/enable//documents/tccconve.pdf*

UNESCO (1990). *World declaration on education for all and framework for action to meet basic learning needs*. UNESCO Publications.

UNESCO (1994). *Salamanca statement and framework for action on special education needs*. United Nations.

UNESCO (2018). *Review studies of education policies and plans to identify priority aspects for inclusion in line with SDG4*. UNESCO Dhaka Office.

UNICEF (2020) *Multiple indicator cluster survey Bangladesh*. Retrieved from https://www.unicef.org/bangladesh/en/reports/progotir-pathey-bangladesh

UNICEF & CIPRB (2023). *Baseline survey in 24 experimental schools*. UNICEF.

WIPO (2023). *Intellectual property statistical country profile*. WIPO.

2
LOOKING BACK, LOOKING FORWARD
Progressing inclusive education

Suzanne Carrington

Introduction

I love that Joanne Banks calls her podcast *Inclusion Dialogue* because it provokes deep critical reflection and action which is what we need if we want to continue our collective work for inclusive education. Carolyn Shields reminds us, "in dialogue, the emphasis is on listening carefully and attempting to truly understand another's position" (Shields, 2020, p. 14). I love this definition and I use it in my school-based projects where I encourage everyone to be respectful of others but also to be brave, ask questions and challenge each other.

Recently I facilitated teams from countries in the Mekong Region in Southeast Asia to share and critically reflect on their work progressing inclusive education in their various organisations. We took a transformative lens to this work and for each country team presentation, the audience responded to guiding questions such as:

- What was done particularly well? Why? Can it be improved further?
- Where were traditional forms of power and privilege at work in this situation?
- In what ways did the practice replicate the status quo?
- Where did race, socioeconomic class, gender, dis/ability, language or religion
- Show up?
- What was the impact?
- What practices might have improved the outcome?
- What practices could increase the equity impact?
- What, if anything, absolutely should have been different?
- What can we learn from this experience that can inform our future practice?

DOI: 10.4324/9781032705484-3

We established respectful relationships with each other to support our collective and individual work. We wanted our critical reflective work to be continual and in the moment. We wanted to challenge each other to improve our practice for greater equity and inclusion.

Some conversation starters that we used were:

- Have you considered _____?
- One thing you might try is _____.

I suggest that critical thinking and dialogue are vital for progressing inclusive education. Critical thinking has been defined as "purposeful, self-regulatory judgment that results in interpretation, analysis, evaluation, and inference, as well as explanations of the considerations on which that judgment is based" (Abrami et al., 2015, p. 275). The podcast *Inclusion Dialogue* has prompted critical thinking, heated debate between my own colleagues and students about beliefs, values. and practice and even one example of critical thinking and dialogue led to updating Michael Giangreco's much-loved cartoons to remove the "special needs language" (https://cdi.uvm.edu/collection/giangrecocartoons).

Like all my fellow podcasters on *Inclusion Dialogue*, I have spent most of my life advocating for equity and inclusion for people with disabilities with a particular focus on transforming schools. My chapter draws from *Inclusion Dialogue: Season Two, Episode Eight*, where I consider my background as a special education teacher in special schools in Australia and England from 1983 to 1993 and the key events that drove me to be a passionate advocate for inclusive education. I then discuss how my doctoral research informed a lifetime of work in schools working with principals, teachers, parents, and students to support systemic change for inclusive education in many countries around the world. Finally, I describe my recent work on transformative leadership, and collaborative research focused on closing special schools in Australia.

How did I become so passionate about inclusive education?

On completion of my teaching qualification (Diploma of Primary Education and Diploma in Special Education) in 1982, I was appointed at the new Queensland government special school in a rural town (approximately 7,000 population). The school had a teaching principal and one teacher (myself) with approximately 20–25 children between 5 and 16 years of age. I taught the junior class with children aged 5–12 years. The children were either local children from the town or children who travelled to the school by bus from the neighbouring smaller towns. Students were enrolled at the special school because they had a disability, struggled with academic work and/or had challenging behaviour. All the enrolled students in the newly built special school were removed from regular schools. The students were selected by school principals and psychologists from the local regular schools and were then placed in the segregated special school away from their peers and siblings. Their regular teachers may have believed that the students would be better off at a special school because they struggled to be successful in the regular school. Many of the students came from poor families. As a teacher, I purchased shoes regularly for students in my class who arrived on cold frosty mornings in bare feet.

The creation of a special school in this town legitimised the decisions of a group of educators to move a group of young people from their local school to a segregated place – a special school. This placement would have influenced the life chances of these young people (Slee, 2011). Although educators at the time were operating in good faith, Roger Slee reminds us of some hard-hitting implications of these political and cultural decisions.

These decisions:

- establish life trajectories that potentially limit opportunities;
- may separate children from their siblings, neighbourhood peers and communities;
- impact upon the nature and quality of the education they engage in;
- reinforce hierarchies that fracture communities and limit human potential;
- have profound economic and health implications for people's future lives;
- may put the interests of institutions above the interests of individuals; and
- compromise our democratic ideal (Slee, 2011, p. 70).

In a small town these "special school students" were labelled and ostracised. They were labelled as "retards". The young people were seen as mentally and physically inadequate. In a small country town – can you imagine the impact on their lives?

For many years it was assumed that children with a disability are better placed in special education settings, but there is no evidence to support this belief (Hehir et al., 2016). Evidence instead demonstrates that placement in segregated settings for children with disabilities has resulted in a marginalised population that has been institutionalised, undereducated, socially rejected, and excluded from society (ACIE, 2020; Biklen, 1988).

The segregation of students in the small town often caused more problems with student behaviour. I am sure that in the peer group circles of the town, "the special school students" were labelled and ostracised in some way. The teenage boys would often be absent from the special school and preferred to be pig hunting, kangaroo shooting or travelling with family in the double-decker, three trailer trucks used to carry sheep and cattle in rural Queensland. These young men were very capable in their various roles outside school and they needed a school curriculum that was more aligned with their interests and the context of living in a rural environment.

In this small town, a group of educators had the power to socially construct a group of young people as disabled enough to send them to a special school.

In 1985 I became a teacher at a special school that was attached to an institution in North QLD, Australia. Many children had significant disabilities and lived in the institution. The children were wards of the state- their parents had been told to forget about them. The children slept in dormitories with beds/cots crowded into one room. They were lined up in the morning in their wheelchairs for teachers to collect them from the institution and wheelchair or walk them to the school on the same grounds as the institution. The children were literally fed like animals by the nursing staff in the institution: children were often seated in buggy-type wheelchairs and the nurses used to tilt the buggy chairs backwards, so the children were seated in an almost horizontal position. This enabled the nurses to feed mushy food to the children quickly. It was distressing to watch, and the teachers and therapists tried to intervene and support more appropriate and caring mealtime practice.

Most of the children developed self-stimulatory behaviour such as rocking and banging their heads due to boredom, anxiety, unhappiness or through copying their peers. In an institution, self-stimulation was normal. The children's cognitive, physical and social and emotional development was clearly stunted and affected by their life living in an institution.

This was only 39 years ago!

These types of experiences highlighted to me, the need for children to be in an inclusive, loving, and caring environment, living with their family in their own community. As a young teacher, I tried to work for more progress and continually challenged the dehumanising aspects of institutional living.

In 1989 I taught at a special school in London, England where I had an early childhood class and the children lived at home with their parents in high-rise apartment blocks and travelled to school every day on a special school bus. They had little contact with children who did not have disabilities, so they all copied each other's inappropriate behaviours!

These children all had delayed language, cognitive impairment, difficulties with social skills, and behaviour challenges. Their schooling also impacted their life opportunities like the children at the special school in the rural town in QLD. These experiences in special schools in Australia and England reinforced my belief that children with disability should be included in regular schools. I knew that there was a need for special education teachers like me to work collaboratively with regular school teachers in one education system, rather than continuing with a dual system of special and regular schools. I believed that the resources allocated to special schools could support a more inclusive education for everyone.

When I returned to work in Australia, I worked in schools in Cairns in Queensland, Australia (1990–1992). The government education department in Cairns closed the special school in 1989, driven by parent advocacy for what was then called integration. Integration is a process of placing students with disabilities in regular education with special education support so the students can adjust to the standardised requirements of the school and classroom. Whereas, inclusion involves a process of systematic reform so that curriculum content, pedagogy, the environment and supports required, respond to barriers to learning and social participation (United Nations, 2016). All the students, teachers, nursing staff, therapists and teacher aides were transferred to local primary and secondary schools in Cairns to support a new process of education for students with disabilities.

Each of these schools had a special education unit within the regular school and was led by a Teacher in Charge. These roles became known as Head of Special Education. The previous school principal of the special school was given a mentoring principal role, and she supported the regular school principals who had enrolled the students with disability, the Heads of Special Education staff, who were implementing collaborative practice to support teachers and students, and supported parent partnerships.

Looking back on this exciting time, I would describe the primary school in Cairns as an inclusive school. The school principal was open and welcoming to all parents and children, including children with complex learning needs. Many children had significant learning and care needs in communication, behaviour, academic learning, and self-care needs. Special education and regular teachers worked together to teach all students in regular classrooms. We had a special education unit that was in an accessible area of the school so children and teachers could access resources and equipment including accessible bathrooms when required. Parents were an important part of the school community.

At this school we moved away from Individual Education Programmes (IEPs) because we knew that regular teachers had many students with diverse needs in their classes and that the IEP process of planning did not work well. The teachers told us that we need to find a different way of working so that they could plan to meet the needs of the whole class. Special education teachers and regular classroom teachers worked collaboratively to make adjustments to the curriculum and pedagogy to meet all students' needs. Not every teacher was committed to those new ideas of practice, but we started working with the teachers who were committed and who were interested in developing new ways of working. Our focus was on supporting students in our local community, which is what inclusive education is, about. In an inclusive approach, students come to school with their siblings and with their neighbours. The teaching staff, therapists, and school leaders just considered what we needed to do to support the students to be successful and to be connected to the school.

There was no clear inclusive education policy and much of the approach at this school was driven by parent advocacy who had a vision of a more inclusive society for their children. I always say that I learnt about being inclusive from that group of parents. I was working in partnership with parents and they gently, and sometimes not so gently, gave me constructive feedback to help me unlearn my special education ways of thinking, and special education practices. The parents would constructively give me feedback about the language that I was using about their children and their education programmes. For example, one day I said, "the children with disabilities can come *down to the special education unit*". A parent said to me, "why do you say *down to the special education unit*"? It is not down a hill". I am not sure why I said those words but on reflection, it may because of my special education deficit thinking about disability. I remember that it was really challenging. In these years of progressing inclusion, I had to challenge my assumptions and ways of thinking that were very special education-focused.

When we consider inclusive education practices today there is a strong focus and expectation of working with stakeholders in a school community: listening to the voice of students; working in partnership with parents; valuing parents' perspective; working in collaborative, democratic ways; having those critical dialogues; and developing those shared sets of values. Developing a shared vision for inclusive education is so important.

At this time, the Queensland government built many special education units in regular primary and secondary schools to support the integration of students with disability. They were called SEUs. However, many of these SEUs were built in the back corner of schools and in many cases operated as segregated settings. They were often fenced and had locked gates, supposedly to keep the students with disabilities safe. A young boy with a disability commented to me:

> If the doors were left open – it would attract more people to come into the SEU. But the doors are closed which makes people feel afraid of the different people inside.

What type of message does this send to the students with disability?

What type of message does this send to students who do not have disability?

The message could be something like this: People with disabilities are a problem and need to be locked up and controlled. It perpetuates the feelings that people with disability are viewed with distaste and fear. These ideas are the same ideas as the views about people with disability from the 1800s.

The bureaucratic decision to build what is most likely seen as safe environments for students with disability drags us backwards and away from progressing inclusive education.

After that time, I started my PhD and, and I was interested to explore what it meant to have an inclusive school culture (Carrington, 2000). An inclusive school culture is one in which school members believe in the "dignity and worth" of all members (United Nations, 2006, Preamble). School culture includes beliefs, values, habits and assumed ways of doing things among the school community. I was interested in the link between beliefs, values and practice, and how that influenced a school in terms of its culture (Carrington, 1999). I also understood that school leaders were vital to leading an inclusive school culture.

Ainscow (1996) argued that in addressing the notion of improved school development, the culture of the school affected the differences in the way schools operated and in the way problems were solved. In my doctoral thesis, I gathered data about beliefs, values, and practices in schools. I noted that there were different patterns of relations between staff and students that affected the amount and type of cooperation and collaboration that occurred and differences in motivation and confidence which affected the problem-solving required in working with students with disabilities.

Transformative school leadership

Research indicates that it is the school leaders who play critical roles in promoting and creating values and conditions that facilitate and support inclusion (DeMatthews et al., 2020). Each national, regional, and local context is different, but every principal can help create and support an inclusive school.

Both listening to students' and parents' voices and supporting collaborative practices, as we did in the school in Cairns, QLD will create spaces for school communities to work together for long-term commitment and change. Such long-term commitment requires ethical leadership to support collaboration, critical inquiry, and transformation in schools. I suggest that the goal of creating inclusive schools should not just focus on supporting students with disabilities but also should be embedded in a broader context of respect for and celebration of difference (Carrington, 1999).

More recently I have been working with a range of school communities to support transformative leaders to create and sustain more inclusive and equitable schools and have published several papers and articles about this work (e.g. Carrington, 2022a,b, 2023). The projects have ranged from six weeks to year-long projects with weekly workshops, readings, workbook activities, and critical dialogue. The project outcomes indicate evidence of shifts in beliefs and practice to support inclusion and a commitment to transformative change for greater equity and inclusion.

These school-based projects are informed by the work of Carolyn Shields (2020) and include a critical perspective so that school leaders, teachers and teacher assistants challenge inequity in everything they think and do. Shields (2014) describes transformative leadership as a critical approach that is focused on promoting equity and inclusion underpinned by inclusive values and beliefs that inform how leaders think and lead. School leaders have a transformational role that can impact individuals and the collective of staff, students, and parents in their school community by developing relationships that are equitable, caring, and open. A transformative leadership approach requires collaboration and inclusive governing structures to address inequity and fosters an inclusive school culture (Cooper, 2009). Leaders who are committed to enact equity need to be activist-oriented and morally transformative (Dantley & Tillman, 2006). This type of approach is required for school leaders wanting to establish an inclusive school culture (Carrington, 1999).

Next steps

We have a growing body of international evidence about the impact on a child, starting school and progressing through an inclusive education pathway, in comparison to a segregated special education pathway (De Bruin, 2024). However, in Australia, there is still a significant amount of our education funding going into building special schools. We seem to have many good policies focused on progressing inclusion but commitment to special education and segregation continues across Australia (Carrington et al., 2022; Lassig et al., 2022).

Our challenges in Australia in progressing a national system of inclusive education are similar to what is happening in other parts of the world (Banks, 2021). There are many advocates and educators questioning the educational and moral premise of segregated schooling (e.g. Slee, 2018). My current collaborative work with researchers from the Centre for Inclusive Education is focused on closing special schools. We suggest that a dual system of mainstream and special schools is hindering the reform that is necessary to create a national inclusive education system in Australia, and we suggest that special schools, in and of themselves, remain a significant barrier to true inclusive education reform. We propose that educational desegregation must occur concurrently with systemic reform supporting inclusion so that all students can be genuinely included.

Our team's most recent publication, closing special schools: lessons from Canada (Mann et al., 2023) draws on a critical review of the Canadian literature documenting the move to inclusion that focused on diminishing special education and closing special schools to some extent. We developed a conceptual framework of drivers for and barriers to special school closure. Drivers and barriers were identified at four levels: (1) societal level, (2) system level, (3) school level and (4) community level. We suggest that the findings will inform policy implementation in countries striving to progress in inclusive education.

Conclusion

This chapter has enabled me to critically reflect on my personal history in starting as a special education teacher and becoming a strong advocate for inclusive education. The chapter has provided a great opportunity for me to document my personal experiences and learning over forty years. I have also shared more recent work that I hope continues to support systemic change for greater inclusion and equity in schools. I hope that this chapter along with the other chapters in the book continue to support critical dialogue to enable challenging the status quo of education that perpetuates inequity and disadvantage and reimagining of education for all in the future.

References

Abrami, P. C., Bernard, R. M., Borokhovski, E., Waddington, D. I., Wade, C. A., & Persson, T. (2015). Strategies for teaching students to think critically: A meta-analysis. *Review of Educational Research, 85*(2), 275–314.

Ainscow, M. (1996). *Inclusion how do we measure up?* Paper presented at A Seminar and Forum on Inclusive Education, Bardon, Brisbane, 26 April, 1996.

Australian Coalition for Inclusive Education (ACIE). (2020). *Driving change: A roadmap for achieving inclusive education in Australia*. Retrieved from https://acie105204494.files.wordpress.com/2020/04/acie-roadmap-final_july-2020.pdf

Banks, J. (2021). A winning formula? Funding inclusive education in Ireland. In J. Goldan, J. Lambrecht, & T. Loreman (Eds.), *Resourcing inclusive education* (pp. 7–19). Emerald Publishing Limited. https://doi.org/10.1108/S1479-363620210000015003

Biklen, D. (1988). The myth of clinical judgment. *Journal of Social Issues*, *44*(1), 127–140.
Carrington, S. (1999). Inclusion needs a different school culture. *International Journal of Inclusive Education*, *3*(3), 257–268.
Carrington, S. (2000). *Accommodating the needs of diverse learners: the impact of teachers' beliefs on classroom practice*. PhD Thesis. School of Education, The University of Queensland. https://espace.library.uq.edu.au/view/UQ:286318
Carrington, S. (2022). Transformative leadership for equity and inclusion. *The Learning Difficulties Australia Bulletin*, *54*(2), 36–38, 1 September 2022 [Featured article].
Carrington, S. (2023). Leadership for equity in schools. *International Encyclopedia of Education (Fourth Edition)*, 401–409. https://doi.org/10.1016/B978-0-12-818630-5.05003-X
Carrington, S., Lassig, C., Maia-Pike, L., Mann, G., Mavropoulou, S., & Saggers, B. (2022). Societal, systemic, school and family drivers for and barriers to inclusive education. *Australian Journal of Education*, *66*(3), 251–264.
Cooper, C. W. (2009). Performing cultural work in demographically changing schools: Implications for expanding transformative leadership frameworks. *Educational Administration Quarterly*, *45*, 694–724.
Dantley, M., & Tillman, L. C. (2006). Social justice and moral transformative leadership. In C. Marshall & M. Oliva (Eds.), *Leadership for social justice: Making revolutions in education* (pp. 16–30). Pearson Education.
De Bruin, K. (2024). Inclusive education. A review of the evidence. In L. Graham (Ed.), *Inclusive education for the 21st century. Theory, policy, and practice* (pp. 95–115). Routledge.
DeMatthews, D., Billingsley, B., McLeskey, J., & Sharma, U. (2020). Principal leadership for students with disabilities in effective inclusive schools. *Journal of Educational Administration*, *58*(5), 539–554.
Hehir, T., Grindal, T., Freeman, B., Lamoreau, R., Borquaye, Y., & Burke, S. (2016). *A summary of the evidence on inclusive education*. Alana Institute.
Lassig, C., Poed, S., Mann, G., Saggers, B., Carrington, S., & Mavropoulou, S. (2022). The future of special schools in Australia: Complying with the convention on the rights of persons with disabilities. *International Journal of Inclusive Education*. https://doi.org/10.1080/13603116.2021.2020344
Mann, G., Carrington, S., Lassig, C., Mavropoulou, S., Saggers, B., Poed, S., & Killingly, C. (2023) Closing special schools: Lessons from Canada. *The Australian Educational Researcher*. https://doi.org/10.1007/s13384-023-00661-5
Shields, C. (2014). Ethical leadership: A critical transformative approach. In C. M. Branson & S. J. Gross (Eds.), *Handbook of ethical educational leadership* (pp. 24–42). Routledge.
Shields, C. (2020). *Becoming a transformative leader: A guide to creating equitable schools*. Routledge.
Slee, R. (2011). *The Irregular school. Exclusion, schooling and inclusive education* (1st ed.). Routledge. https://doi.org/10.4324/9780203831564
Slee, R. (2018). *Inclusive education isn't dead, it just smells funny*. Routledge. https://doi.org/10.4324/9780429486869
United Nations (2006). *Convention on the rights of persons with disabilities*. United Nations.
United Nations (2016). General Comment No 4, Article 24: Right to Inclusive Education. (CRPD/C/GC/4). https://digitallibrary.un.org/record/1313836?ln=en

3
A PERSONAL REFLECTION ACROSS DECADES OF EDUCATION

Chris Forlin

Training as a teacher

I am now living in Western Australia (WA), although I was born in London. I trained as a teacher in the late 1960s. I was living in Southampton and did my final practicum training on the Isle of Wight. When we qualified in England, we were able to select one or two districts that we wanted to go to complete our probationary year, and then the government allocated you to a school. I had selected London, and the London Borough of Brent and I was allocated to a primary school in a very low socio-economic area. At that stage, London was just opening to international families coming from the Americas as migrants. We had a lot of West Indies immigrants, and our school was one of the few schools that were taking them. This was quite an experience as the welcome was not overly positive by Londoners.

I had 50 students aged 7–8 years in my class. They all sat at long desks next to each other - the ones with the big pop-up tops, and the inkwell in the corner. To move around the room, you had to climb across the seats. On day one I had a big desk out the front, which you stepped up to, and on my desk, there was a cane, and one piece of chalk. When that chalk was used right down to nothing, I was allowed to ask for another piece. The children had inkwells, and you had an inkwell monitor, and oh my goodness, what a mess that used to be!

Experiencing cultural diversity

As I reflect on special education, at that stage the variety of needs of the children in my classroom was mainly due to cultural differences. We had no support, there were no additional staff involved. There was no training and, as a new teacher, you literally went into the classroom and did whatever you liked provided you maintained some form of control.

DOI: 10.4324/9781032705484-4

From that early beginning, where I got to see and experience a whole range of issues, and inclusion from a cultural perspective, this has always underpinned my approach towards including all learners. As the new immigrants were not welcomed by the community, there was very much a divide between the two. In the very tight classrooms, though, there was no room for a divide, they were all mixed in together, and the children accepted it. Unfortunately, the parents didn't. That was my first real exposure to diversity.

My training was very different from current preservice teacher training. It was a full-time three-year course. For us, full-time meant we were scheduled for eight-hour days from 8.30, with a one-hour lunch break, in classes or lectures or working with children. There was no time to work outside of college. In that respect, we did have a lot of hands-on practical activities for preparing us for teaching. In a way, I believe we were more prepared for the skills of teaching. What we didn't have, though, was an understanding of the differences in children as the expectation was 'there's your class, they're all the same, you all read the same book, and on the same page'. Everyone was expected to write the same work on their note pad. There was no consideration at all for differences within a regular classroom. As this was the accepted norm for regular schools, teachers did not really question this. Students were graded according to ability across year groups (labelled, e.g. 2A, 2B, 2C and 2D) and within classes and often were asked to stand and call out the position they held in the class from first to 50th!

Following my probationary year and now being fully qualified as a teacher, I decided to go overseas. I was married at the time, and we applied through the British Consulate. As a Commonwealth country, we were sent to Zambia in Africa. That was another completely different diverse look at life. Only my husband could get a contract because women weren't allowed to, unless they were single and going on their own. I was, therefore, employed locally. The other teachers in the school were either locals or many of the wives of the expats who were out there. They had no qualifications whatsoever. Consequently, education was extremely poor, haphazard, and mainly a babysitting role, leaving the children very poorly educated.

I found that experience very interesting; I really enjoyed the three years, and it gave me a great understanding of the importance of quality training of teachers. At the end of the contract, there was an option to take another contract. At this stage, though, there were a number of challenges living so close to the northern border. We also had our first daughter at the end of the contract and decided we should move on. Most people leaving were either going to Australia or to Canada but were not going back to England. As I much prefer the heat to the cold we went to Australia and this is where I got into special education.

My Australian journey

When I arrived in Australia in the early 70s, I obviously had no Australian teaching background. This made it extremely difficult to get a job teaching in a school without doing a required rural two-year stint in a remote school (which wasn't viable with my husband's job in the city). The only schools that would offer me casual employment were special schools because they found it very difficult to find willing trained teachers. I gradually realised that these schools appealed to me. Not only did I like working in special schools, but I found being able to really focus on individual children and support those who were seen as 'different' was very motivating for me. As soon as a child was identified with a mild disability or learning difficulty, they were moved to a special school. The range of abilities was, therefore, quite broad. At that stage, many children with high and profound support needs were still not in schools at all, being completely excluded, or placed in residential institutions. I then went on to lead a kindergarten in Victoria. I wasn't kindergarten trained, but as a willing and trained teacher, I was given the role as a principal of a Spastic Society (sic) kindergarten. Nowadays, these terms are just not acceptable, but at the time, that was what was used. That is how I moved into special education. Once you get into it, you get hooked. Absolutely.

Returning to the homeland and back again to special education!

Eventually, after five years in Queensland and Victoria we returned to England for a couple of years. We quickly decided it really wasn't what we wanted, so we moved back to Perth in WA. Again, I had the same problems. I couldn't get into a regular school because at that stage teaching in WA, to get a permanent job or to get a job where you wanted, you had to have completed what was called 'country practice', which was two years wherever the department wanted to send you. I now had a young family of three, and a husband, who was working in Perth, so I couldn't go 'out bush'. I ended up not being able to acquire a permanent job for about eight or 10 years before I had a full-time contracted local job. It was the women that were the ones who were doing contract work, leaving a very unstable teaching situation. As I now had some background in special schools, and permanent teachers mainly still did not want to teach in them, these were the only contracts that I was offered.

I have to say, though, that at this stage, I really enjoyed working in the special schools. It was working with the more challenging students, and the staff there was genuinely caring and sensitive to student needs. The staff attitudes were not patronising, like I found later when I was working in Asia. The downside was that the curriculum wasn't academic, with students learning practical and community-based skills, which was the focus at the time.

The start of integration

Thinking back to my English experience and reading the research that was coming out from there, the move towards integration in the early 80s was starting to take hold in England but was just being talked about in Australia (Beazley, 1984; Karmel Report, 1973; Shean, 1993), national legislation of rights in 2005 by the Disability Standards for Education (Chambers & Forlin, 2021a). Australia tended to follow what was happening in England in its progressive move towards originally integration and then eventually nearly three decades later, inclusion. Comparing WA to schools in Zambia, though, was so different. In Zambia, there was nothing remotely like integration occurring. Most children who had a disability were kept isolated at home. If a child could not get to school, or and couldn't learn or behave like their peers, they were not educated. There were no options available and no possibility of receiving a differentiated curriculum.

In the mid-80s, I managed to secure a position in a Language Development Centre in WA. It was really a 'special school' for children with delayed and disordered language, although it was situated on the site of a regular school. The Government intention was for the children to be integrated. However, like most other education support centres at that time, our children were not allowed to mix at all with students in the regular school, having to take separate breaks and being restricted to their own playground areas.

While there, the principal's position became vacant. I had been there for about six years, and I was the most experienced, but I wasn't allowed to apply because I didn't have a degree. When I started my teacher training, there were no education degrees, just diplomas. Consequently, in the early 1990s, I studied further at university for my BEd (Hons 1st.) and then my doctorate. I was very interested in the lack of genuine inclusion, so that became my focus. This led to the start of my second career.

My second career

After completing my doctorate in inclusive education (Forlin, 1995; Forlin & Cole, 1993), I decided that I could contribute my years of experience and broad knowledge by training teachers in this still very new area. Over the next 10 years, I worked in universities in Queensland and WA in this evolving field. My research and publication focus were on enhancing the move towards inclusion, finding myself working internationally with many like-minded colleagues, and developing life-long partnerships and friends.

My Asian experience

In 2005, I accepted a position at the Education University of Hong Kong (EDUHK). I found this experience very rewarding for several reasons. Firstly, because Hong Kong schools weren't inclusive, and, secondly, because there were so many children there who were unable to access any education to meet their needs. This provided a great opportunity for me to support Hong Kong and other Asian countries (Forlin, 2007a, 2007b), in understanding the concept of inclusion and in establishing inclusive policies and practices to facilitate it. This also gave me a wonderful opportunity to travel around Asia and internationally, and to experience their education systems and understand how they were educating students with special needs.

(e.g. Forlin, 2011, 2019; Romero-Contrerasa et al., 2013). This gave me a huge insight into a range of different cultural understandings of inclusive education, and the local challenges faced by systems trying to adopt international expectations to become more inclusive of learners with special educational needs (Chambers & Forlin, 2021a).

Most of the Asian countries I visited were starting to use the term, 'an integrated approach to inclusive education', which is somewhat of an enigma as these concepts are quite different. They would refer to 'inclusion' as any form of education, where a child with a disability was placed, either in the regular school, or in a special class, within the regular school. Throughout Asia, every country has a different interpretation and understanding of inclusion. If a child was registered in a regular school, they were called the 'inclusion child'. In most instances, this did not entitle them to any additional support, and this term was both isolating and highlighted the child's problems. In many ways, it was used as an excuse for the child not being able to maintain progress with their peers. In addition, a child identified with a special need could only be included if they were able to cope with the regular lessons without any modification or additional support.

Teachers across Asia were traditionally employed based on their ability to help students pass the regulated exams. Students needed to do well, otherwise, the teachers were blamed, often resulting in the loss of their jobs. In 2005 in Hong Kong, there was a five-level hierarchy of secondary schools, and students were allocated according to their ability (Forlin, 2019). This reminded me of the classroom grading system I experienced back in the 50s and 60s in the UK, where depending on your ability, you were assigned a level. These schools were not only following that antiquated model, but it was being implemented at a whole school level. Once allocated to a school level, there was very little chance of improving. Teachers were also allocated to a school level depending on their students' exam results. Based purely on examination results, the top schools were given the best teachers, resources, and equipment! The less capable students had the least opportunities to achieve with the weaker teachers. After I arrived, the government reduced the five levels to just three, which was promoted as being an incredible advancement in education.

When discussing inclusion in Asia, all children with any special need were only found in level three schools – if they were even 'included'. For parents who fought to enrol their child with a special learning need into a regular school, the children were confronted with an inflexible curriculum, high demands on achieving good examination results, extensive homework requirements, and the need for the child to finish work not completed at school. In addition, the parents often paid for private tutoring. It was not uncommon for children to still be awake after 11 o'clock at night to finish their work. At this stage, many special schools existed throughout Asia, with most being operated by philanthropic associations.

During my time in Asia, one of my most interesting research areas was in investigating the attitudes, sentiments, concerns, and efficacy of teachers working in these new, more diverse classrooms (e.g. Chao et al., 2016; Correia et al., 2019; Kuok et al., 2020).

In collaboration with a range of international colleagues, over a period of many years we developed a set of scales to measure teachers' perceptions about inclusion (Forlin et al., 2011; Sharma et al., 2012). These scales continue to be widely adopted in 2023, with similar findings across an extensive range of countries. Over time, teachers reported increased positive sentiments and attitudes towards inclusion, but their concerns remain linked with unrealistic systemic expectations, crowded classrooms (especially across Asia and Africa), and their perceived inability to provide highly effective interventions and support for all learners.

How has inclusion changed?

When leaving Hong Kong in 2015, it was evident that since arriving there a decade earlier, the move towards a more inclusive approach to education was being taken seriously (Chao et al., 2016; Forlin, 2007, 2019). Most countries had developed national policies, with many interpreting these into regional legislation and school-based policies. Across Asia, there was a concerted effort at all levels to better train teachers about inclusive education; and teachers had become familiar with the term (Forlin, 2019; Forlin & Sin, 2010). Teachers talked about inclusive education as the way forward, as recommended by the governments. However, the expectation for students to participate in the same curriculum remained, although teachers were expected to show evidence of modifications and support. The most common approach was to withdraw students to special classes and/or enrol them in extra classes after school. The teachers were very supportive and dedicated their own time, in addition to their heavy workloads. The downside was that in the extra classes the students were only coached in the same class curriculum, which they hadn't learned in the regular class, the goal being to improve their exam results.

Another area of personal interest was that while significant research was published across the first two decades of the millennium about inclusive education and the ways that countries were addressing the international declarations, there remained little research that listened to the voices of the children with special needs, considering their experiences and desires. I am pleased to say in the last five years there has been a much stronger focus on this across most jurisdictions, resulting in some very useful outcomes that can help teachers to identify and address the concerns students continue to raise. Our own research supported the international findings and led to this area becoming a key area of focus for pre-service teacher training in Hong Kong, Macau and other Asian countries.

Meanwhile, inclusion in most well-developed countries including Australia has led to significant changes in educational philosophy and parental choice. All states and territories in Australia now provide options for schooling based on the requests of the parents (Chambers & Forlin, 2021a, 2021b). In some regions, special schools have been relocated to shared sites or even closed completely. Parents have much greater control in decision-making, and if they want their child to experience inclusion in their local mainstream school, regardless of the child's level of need, schools are required to support this decision (Disability Discrimination Act; Standards for Education 2005). Extensive national support structures are in place, such as the National Consistent Collection of Data (NCCD) (Sharma et al., 2019) to ensure an appropriate level of support for all learners with an identified additional learning need (ALN). To register as a teacher, the Australian Professional Standards for Teachers (Australian Institute for Teaching and School Leadership) requires that graduates '…demonstrate broad knowledge and understanding of legislative requirements and teaching strategies that support participation and learning of students with disability' (p. 11). Conversely, in most Asian countries, expectations for students with special needs remain the same as their peers. Minor modifications are made (e.g. extra time), but they still have to follow the same curriculum and pass the same exams.

Emerging from COVID

At the time of this interview countries were just beginning to emerge from COVID. This had undoubtedly impacted enormously on most students, but specifically on those with moderate to high learning needs. During the previous year when many systems experienced the need for online teaching, I had been working with colleagues from the Philippines. In attempting to summarise the current situation regarding the impact of COVID on inclusion, they coined the term VUCA (Volatile, Uncertain, Complex, Ambiguous [VUCA]).

A volatile, uncertain, complex, ambiguous (VUCA) approach to inclusion

In 2022, my colleagues from the Philippines produced a complete volume dedicated to how countries are coping with VUCA (Narot & Kiettikunwong, 2023). This insightful book on interdisciplinary perspectives considers the many changes that are occurring that impact directly inclusive education. While concluding that such major educational interruptions, such as COVID, are challenging for all systems, these were identified as being even more challenging when aiming to provide effective teaching and learning for children and youth with special and diverse needs and disabilities.

Volitivity

While schools have always experienced a constant state of change, this has been elevated to an unprecedented level during COVID. Even though by 2023, most systems had returned to the status quo of on-campus schooling, the volatility of education continues. In Australia, this is compounded by the different education systems in each state and territory, and the challenges faced by trying to implement more national approaches to ensuring the needs of students with ALN are met in a more equitable way across diverse regions.

Uncertainty

Like educational volitivity, many regions continue to live through unpredictable and uncertain times. In WA, we had not yet emerged completely from lockdown during this interview and were considered a closed state. We still did not know when we were going to open for international travel when students were going to be sent home because of new cases of COVID in a school, as everything was very unpredictable. People were trying to get back to a 'new normal' but were still not able to plan with any certainty.

Complexity

Complexity in education is also far broader than just COVID. Without a doubt, there has been an enormous increase in the diversity and different types of student needs, especially during the past decade. Aligned with this has been the increase in expectation for teachers. One area that has emerged significantly has been the number of students who are presenting with severe emotional and behavioural disorders, including depression, anxiety, and physical violence. While COVID highlighted mental health issues, these concerns have been increasing exponentially across the past decade. This is particularly the case with disenfranchised students, causing serious problems for schools that have been unable to safely include them (Jones et al., 2023). Since the millennium, it has become the norm for students with disabilities to be accepted into regular schools, either within regular classes or within on-site support centres. With the increase in the number of students with aggressive behaviours, schools are moving this new cohort in reverse, seeking alternative placements for them outside the regular school. Nationally, we have seen a plethora of 'new' (special) schools emerge named to avoid stigmatisation, such as 'care schools', 'drop in schools', just to avoid the title of special school; but ultimately, they are just segregated schools. This diversity of student needs is a huge issue. If we do not come to terms with this quickly, we are going to revert to a new, but undoubtedly still a different type, of 'special education'.

Ambiguity

Not only is the term 'equity' somewhat ambiguous, but so too is the term 'inclusive education'. Unless we can define both, addressing these will remain challenging and unattainable. One of the big issues we have in Australia, which may not be the same for you, is ensuring equity across the divide between urban and rural education. We have families living thousands of kilometres away from major cities in isolated or small communities, trying to achieve the same outcomes as our students in urban cities. Acquiring support is challenging, although online resources have improved the situation. I think we need to keep focusing on that.

At the same time, we have found that there has been a noticeable increase in parents choosing to home-school their children. Before COVID, there was anecdotal evidence regarding the increasing number of students being educated at home, rather than attending school. This became a real research interest for my colleagues and I, especially as to how this relates to the move towards inclusive education in local schools. Based on an extensive review of the research literature, we developed the *Parents' Perceptions of Home-schooling* (PPHS) scale for measuring the diversity of motivations and practices of home-schooling (Forlin et al., 2023). We found that in Europe, particularly in the Republic of Ireland, home-schooling was increasing particularly for students with disability (Banks et al., 2023). In Australia, data similarly indicated a definite increase in the number of home-schooling families and that decisions were based on either proactive or reactive reasons (Forlin & Chambers, 2023). The latter was particularly pertinent for children with disability or ADL.

Moving forward

At this stage, it might be opportune to reflect on potential futures for special and inclusive education. With the existing VUCA challenges any discussions surrounding this are going to be subjective based on local contexts and cultures. I think we need to remain very cognisant that the four VUCA issues are going to continue, and that we need to address them upfront. Certainly, in less developed countries, we need to work on improving the knowledge and understanding of inclusive education – teachers, leaders, and systems. All regions also need better trained teachers and more specifically qualified and well-trained teacher educators. I think there needs to be much greater reliability on leaders in schools, as currently many of them can opt-out by delegating the role of supporting learners with special needs to Learning Support Coordinators.

We also need to monitor student outcomes much more closely by focusing on what we are trying to achieve and whether the outcomes that we have selected are appropriate. There has been a big push in Australia for helping learners with high support needs to develop more practical skills so that they are prepared for entering the workforce, rather than sitting at home and not being able to be employed. A plethora of providers have emerged offering a range of postschool options to address this. As with a curriculum that needs to be followed by all students, the regular class curriculum is no longer focused on a life-skills approach for these students.

Regardless of the form that schools of the future will take, there will remain aspects of education that will be constant. There will always be children for whom society needs to provide an education. Students will need to be motivated to learn and have more opportunities to engage with the newest technologies. Teachers (or newly structured enablers) will be responsible, whether it is face-to-face, online, or through some other method of virtual technology. Funding will never be sufficient, and resources will remain inadequate.

Support approaches will need to adapt to the new structure of schooling. Greater accountability will be placed on education providers to support learners with increasing diversity and decreasing emotional stability. It will be important to raise the status of teaching to ensure people will take on an even more eclectic, complex, and advancing role. Teacher education will need to become more flexible, and the curriculum to have the capacity to evolve more efficiently to meet the needs of the rapidly changing learning environment.

The curriculum will need to be facilitated through a pedagogy that is going to change dramatically. Most importantly, the physical 'school' as it is now, is unlikely to exist. The debate about inclusive education will no longer be around physical placement per se and access to education, as a range of options will ensure all students are able to learn in the way that suits them best. Developing social structures that allow for individuality while endeavouring to maintain cohesive societies, will, however, become increasingly challenging as more isolated options for learning, and less engagement in face-to-face situations become the norm.

Providing educational equity will remain a key dispute regarding how limited sources can be shared equitably between mounting numbers of diverse groups of learners. Issues surrounding which placement options should receive the limited funding and resources are likely to become the new dialogue in the context of including all learners.

Conclusion

A key question to ask in conclusion to this reflection is how do schools know when they are getting better at inclusive education and that what they are doing is working? Schools need to be made more accountable by providing data and evidence that demonstrates the outcomes they are citing. The importance of measuring progress toward inclusive education (Forlin & Loreman, 2014), and the need for effective resourcing (Goldan et al., 2021), continue to be highlighted in research. When I took over as Series Editor of the *International Perspectives on Inclusive Education* in 2014, the first volume I produced together with Tim Loreman, addressed the topic of how to measure the impact and effectiveness of inclusive education. The issues raised in that volume, and the call for greater accountability through comparable measures, remain today. As espoused following a detailed analysis of the education of learners with disabilities in WA over the past half century, we concluded the following:

> The next 50 years are likely to see an even greater, exponential transformation in the provision of, and access to, schooling for students with disability. Will the seminal work of Rawls, undertaken 50 years ago, continue to find a place in discussions and educational debates, and contribute to future decision-making for safeguarding equitable educational rights and justice for all learners during the next half century? As the foundation of his philosophy transcends politics and cultural norms and provides an excellent basis for dialogue around equitable access to, and engagement in, education for all students, we certainly hope that it will.
>
> *(Chambers & Forlin, 2021b, p. 16)*

To find out more about my work

Of critical importance is the absolute need to take much greater notice of teachers' concerns. While teachers continue to express that they are insufficiently prepared to cater for the diversity of student need, governments expect them to cater for learners who present with even more complex needs; especially in areas of social-emotional behaviour. To safeguard the rights of all learners to an equitable inclusive education, we must also ensure that teachers have the training and support with access to appropriate resources to enable them to provide effective learning for all.

This chapter includes just a selection of my research to acknowledge the diversity and complexity of inclusive education as it has spanned my academic career. To find out more about my work LinkedIn and Scopus are probably the best for a quick overview, but ResearchGate enables you to request any of my articles. Most recently much of my research is being published in Open Access which makes it easier for more researchers to be able to access them directly.

References

Australian Government (2005). *Disability standards for education 2005 plus guidance notes*. https://www.education.gov.au/swd/resources/disability-standards-education-2005-plus-guidance-notes

Banks, J., Forlin, C., & Chambers, D. (2023). Home-schooling in the Republic of Ireland. *British Journal of Special Education, 50*(3), 394–402. https://doi.org/10.1111/1467-8578.12468

Beazley, K. (1984). *Report of the Committee of Inquiry into Education in Western Australia.* Ministry of Education, Perth, Australia.

Chambers, D., & Forlin, C. (2021a). An historical review from exclusion to inclusion in Western Australia across the past five decades: What have we learnt? *Education Sciences, 11*(119), 1–15. https://doi.org/10.3390/educsci11030119

Chambers, D., & Forlin, C. (2021b). An historical ethnography of the enactment of Rawl's theory of justice as applied to the education of learners with disability in Western Australia. *International Journal of Inclusive Education*. https://doi.org/10.1080/13603116.2021.1941322

Chao, G., Forlin, C., & Ho, F. C. (2016). Improving teaching self-efficacy for teachers in inclusive classrooms in Hong Kong. *International Journal of Inclusive Education*. https://doi.org/10.1080/13603116.2016.1155663

Correia, A., Monteiro, E., Teixeira, V., Kuok, A., & Forlin, C. (2019). The interplay between a Confucian-heritage culture and teachers' sentiments and attitudes towards inclusion in Macau. *European Journal of Special Education Research*, 5(2), 43–61. Available at: https://oapub.org/edu/index.php/ejse/article/view/2729

Forlin, C. (1995). Educators' beliefs about inclusive practices in Western Australia. *British Journal of Special Education*, 22, 179–185.

Forlin, C. (2007a). A collaborative, collegial and more cohesive approach to supporting educational reform for inclusion in Hong Kong. *Asia-Pacific Education Review*, 8(2), 1–11.

Forlin, C. (2007b). Inclusive educational practices: A way forward for Hong Kong. *Chinese Education & Society*, 40(4), 64–77.

Forlin, C. (2011). *Teacher educators supporting inclusive education in Vietnam*. EADSNE Inclusion-in-Action project website. https://www.inclusive-education-in-action.org/case-study/teacher-educators-supporting-inclusive-education-vietnam

Forlin, C. (2019). Teacher education and inclusion in the Asia-Pacific region. In J. Lambert (Ed.), *The Oxford research encyclopedia of education*. Oxford University Press. https://oxfordre.com/education/display/10.1093/acrefore/9780190264093.001.0001/acrefore-9780190264093-e-570

Forlin, C., & Chambers, D. (2023). Is a whole school approach to inclusion really meeting the needs of all learners? Home-schooling parents' perceptions. *Education Sciences*, 13(6). https://doi.org/10.3390/educsci13060571.

Forlin, C., Chambers, D., & Banks, J. (2023). Developing a scale to measure the diversity of motivations and practices of home-schooling. *Educational Review*. https://doi.org/10.1080/00131911.2023.2229067

Forlin, C., & Cole, P. (1993). Attributions of the social acceptance and integration of children with a mild intellectual disability. *Australian and New Zealand Journal of Children With a Developmental Disability*, 19(1), 11–23.

Forlin, C., Earle, C., Loreman, T., & Sharma, U. (2011). The sentiments, attitudes and concerns about inclusive education revised (SACIE-R) scale for measuring pre-service teachers' perceptions about inclusion. *Exceptionality Education International*, 21(2 & 3), 50–65.

Forlin, C., & Loreman, T. (2014). *Measuring inclusive education. international perspectives on inclusive education*, Vol 3. Series Editor Chris Forlin. Emerald.

Forlin, C., & Sin, K. (2010). Developing support for inclusion: A professional learning approach for teachers in Hong Kong. *Journal of Whole Schooling*, 6(1), 7–26. http://www.wholeschooling.net/Journal_of_Whole_Schooling/IJWSIndex.html

Goldan, J., Lambrecht, J., & Loreman, T. (2021). Resourcing inclusive education. *International perspectives on inclusive education*, Vol. 15. Series Editor Chris Forlin. Emerald.

Jones, R., Kreppner, J., & Fiona Marsh, F. (2023). Punitive behaviour management policies and practices in secondary schools: A systematic review of children and young peoples' perceptions and experiences. *Emotional and Behavioural Difficulties*. https://doi.org/10.1080/13632752.2023.2255403

Karmel, P. (1973). *Schools in Australia: Report of the Interim Committee for the Australian Schools Commission, Interim Committee for the Australian Schools Commission*. https://apo.org.au/node/29669

Kuok, A. C. H., Teixeira, V., Forlin, C., Monteiro, E., & Correia, A. (2020). The effect of self-efficacy and role understanding on teachers' emotional exhaustion and work engagement in inclusive education in Macao (SAR). *International Journal of Disability, Development, and Education.* https://doi.org/10.1080/1034912X.2020.1808949

Narot, P., & Kiettikunwong, N. (2023). Interdisciplinary perspective on special and inclusive education in a volatile, uncertain, complex, ambiguous (VUCA) world. *International perspectives on inclusive education*, Vol. 20. Series Editor Chris Forlin. Emerald.

Romero-Contrerasa, S., Garcia-Cedilloa, I., Forlin, C., & Karla Abril Lomelí-Hernándeza, K. (2013). Preparing teachers for inclusion in Mexico: How effective are we? *Journal of Education for Teaching.* http://dx.doi.org/10.1080/02607476.2013.836340

Sharma, U., Furlonger, B., & Forlin, C. (2019). The impact of funding models on the education of students with Autism Spectrum Disorder (ASD). *Australasian Journal of Special Education,* 12, 1–28

Sharma, U., Loreman, T., & Forlin, C. (2012). Measuring teacher efficacy to implement inclusive practices. *Journal of Research in Special Educational, Needs,* *12*(1), 12–21. https://doi.org/10.1111/j.1471-3802.2011.01200.x

Shean, R. (1993). The education of students with disabilities and specific learning difficulties. Report of the State Government Taskforce. Western Australia Ministry of Education, Perth, Australia.

4
WHAT "ALL" MEANS

James M. Kauffman

Personal history

I became a special educator because of my conscientious objection to war. In the spring of 1962, I had completed my undergraduate degree in elementary education at Goshen College in three-and-a-half years and had a semester's teaching experience in a public school in northern Indiana. I knew I would not be drafted, but I decided to volunteer for work qualifying as an alternative to military service. I needed to find a job that would qualify under the U.S.'s *Selective Service Act* (see Akst, 2022; not all conscientious objection to war is based on religion; mine was, is not now).

Under selective service, teaching emotionally disturbed children at the Southard School, then the children's division of the Menninger Psychiatric Clinic in Topeka, Kansas, was an option. The principal of Southard when I applied and was hired in 1962 was the late Richard J. (Dick) Whelan, who later became my advisor at the University of Kansas (see Kauffman, 2015).

After two years of voluntary service at Southard, I also completed a master's degree in teaching in the elementary school. I intended to be a career classroom teacher. However, those who had advised me in my master's program had recommended me for a variety of doctoral programs, and I received applications to apply for admission to several. Dick Whelan asked me to come to Kansas City (I was still living in Topeka) and consider his doctoral program in special education. I have never been sorry that I chose Dick's program.

When I started my career at the University of Virginia (UVA) in 1970, there was no mandatory federal law governing special education. Five years later, there was: the federal mandate called the *Education for All Handicapped Children Act* of 1975 (EAHCA, also often called Public Law 94–142, now known as the *Individuals with*

Disabilities Education Improvement Act, usually called IDEA). Although I was highly skeptical of the federal law for a few years immediately after it was passed (Kauffman, 1980), I eventually recognized its necessity and value (e.g., Kauffman, 1989, 1999–2000, 2022; Martin, 2013). Making special education a Title (a part of another law) rather than a separate law would, in my opinion, be a disaster for most individuals with disabilities.

I have been a special education advocate for more than half a century and see it as an essential part of public education (Anastasiou et al., 2024). Some people manage in some way to consider themselves advocates for children with disabilities by opposing special education (e.g., Baglieri et al., 2011; Connor, 2014; Taylor & Sailor, 2024; Taylor et al., 2024). They typically do so in the name of disability studies (DS) or disability studies in education (DSE), supposing they are working both within and against special education. To me, that is much like trying to work within and against a corrupt administration; it does not go well. If I thought IDEA is dangerous or built on bad or outdated ideas, I would separate myself from it as clearly as possible, and work against it as an outsider.

Working within and against needs clarification. It is one thing to work within an entity one considers legitimate and against specific policies or practices one considers wrong. It is quite another thing to work within and against an entity, one considers illegitimate and in need of destruction. For example, it is one thing to work within the framework of the federal government of the United States but against racism and white supremacy, but it is quite another to work within the United States with the intent of destroying and replacing its federal government, as do domestic terrorists and insurrectionists (e.g., see Stevens, 2023; Toobin, 2023). I work within special education but against its poor practices or malpractice. My intent is improving special education. I do not work within it but against it with the intent of destroying it, undermining it, or delegitimizing it. I believe special education is a legitimate, necessary, and needed part of public education—and always will be.

I continue to see special education as something we must keep and improve if we want all children and youths with disabilities to have the best education we can provide them. I agree with Walker (2003), who said of the category of emotional and behavioral disorders (although I think something very similar could be said of all categories of special education):

> I believe our field stands as a lighthouse beacon of hope, caring and unconditional support for these at-risk children and youth to whom life has dealt such a cruel hand. I have been a researcher in the area of school-related behavior disorders for over three decades. During that time, I have been proud to call myself a member of the field which brings together dedicated professionals from diverse backgrounds who work together so well on behalf of at-risk children. Our field models and demonstrates positive values and best practices that can make a real difference in the lives of children and youth with emotional and behavioral disorders and those of their families.

Special education needs a lot of improvement, even though we are proud to be special educators. Embracing a philosophy or way of thinking about disabilities and educational needs that do not see a specific, separate special education law (not a Title or part of another law) as necessary to make things better for children in school is, in my opinion, unintelligent, deceitful, shameful, and inexcusable.

Word meanings

The meanings and uses of words like "all" (and "always") and "no" (and "none" or "never") and others such as "regular," "special," "general," "mainstream," "inclusion," "segregated," "integrated," "only," and so on have always intrigued me, perhaps because of my philosophical bent and my desire to use language that is as accurate and precise as I can make it, especially in writing. I think it is appropriate to ask what instances (or cases or groups) are included or excluded when, in common parlance, the word "all" is used but is not meant to be taken literally. For example, we might say, "All citizens have the right to vote." True, in a sense, but we understand that some citizens are younger than the voting age, so "all" cannot be taken literally in that statement. We could, of course, say, "All living citizens ___ or older" (or "of legal voting age") have the right to vote." That statement might be taken almost literally, and if any legal exceptions are stated (e.g., convicted felons, people of voting age but not able to indicate their ballot choices independently) then we would have to say something like "almost all" or "most" or admit that "all" is not to be taken truly literally.

Among the greatest problems I see in special education today is someone saying and writing the slogan "all means all"—or, at least accepting the slogan—but claiming *not* to be an advocate of full inclusion. This is self-contradiction of the highest order, an Orwellian nightmare (Orwell, 1954). To me, it is maddening that so many of those saying that *all* children with disabilities or special educational needs should be included in general education, yet admit there are exceptions, but decline to say just how and by whom alternative placements are to be determined. I find it maddening that people do not "come clean" linguistically and say just what they mean. Their words imply that they're not serious or precise thinkers or believe that imprecise language is ok. Their imprecision in thinking and writing or speaking does not serve special education or the individuals it is intended to help. In fact, their imprecision is dangerous.

Greenhouse (2020; see also Greenhouse, 2021), a noted legal scholar, mentioned how imprecise thinking and writing have negative implications for social justice. She noted how a U. S. Supreme Court justice who uses words and concepts imprecisely is frighteningly dangerous. That judge is dangerous because precision in using words is essential in making good law and being able to interpret law accurately. Greenhouse (2020) observed that discrimination, in the sense of unfair treatment, is considered evil by nearly everyone, but that discrimination means treating things that are alike as if they are not. Moreover, discrimination implies that they are treated that way for no good reason. Special educators understand that discrimination also involves treating things that are, in reality, different but as if they are alike. And doing so for no good reason makes such discrimination a pungent evil in education.

This understanding of discrimination explains why the comparison of disability to many other forms of diversity is illogical—unless it is also assumed that disabilities, like skin color, can be made irrelevant simply by removing legal and social barriers. The expectation that removing barriers for people with disabilities will make their disabilities disappear (or render them irrelevant) is a lie maintained by shoddy thinking and misuse of words. Supposing that "separate is inherently unequal" applies to disability as well as to skin color is an example of this kind of shallow, shabby thinking about the meanings of words (e.g., Stainback & Stainback, 1991; see also Harden, 2021). It encourages the witless lumping of disabilities with other forms of diversity as if they all have the exact same or essentially similar implications for teaching or inclusion.

An important issue is what the word inclusion means for students with disabilities (often abbreviated with the acronym SWD). These youngsters are also known as those with special educational needs and disabilities (SEND). We must consider just what "inclusion" means for SWD (or SEND, which I consider the better of the two acronyms) in publicly funded education. Kauffman and Badar (2020) called bodily inclusion *habeas corpus* inclusion because it is concerned with showing (*habeas*) where the student's body (*corpus*) is. We used Latin also to indicate inclusion in appropriate instruction: appropriate or proper (*proprium*) instruction (*instructio*) or *proprium instructio* inclusion. We have argued elsewhere that appropriate instruction is more important than bodily inclusion (e.g., Kauffman & Badar, 2014, 2016), that instruction comes first and where instruction happens is clearly of secondary concern. Of course, it is possible to have *both* habeas corpus inclusion *and* proprium instructio inclusion—*sometimes*. I do not believe having both is *always* possible. And I think "all means all" in the case of *habeas corpus* inclusion is linguistic drive driven by intellectual flaccidity. Henceforth in this chapter, "inclusion" refers to bodily inclusion in general education (i.e., *habeas corpus* inclusion *in education*), not to inclusion of any kind in other activities and contexts. However, inclusion in education is certainly not the same as inclusion in other activities. Probably, nearly everyone agrees that education is the purpose of schools, but there is less unanimity about what counts as education and how schools are different from other environments in a young person's education. Certainly, important education occurs outside of schools. Furthermore, schools reflect society. Schools do not create society. They do not and cannot model what a society should be.

I think the primary purpose of schooling is appropriate instruction in and students' learning of academic and self-help skills. Instruction is not the same as having access to other community activities, and exposure to curriculum and instruction is not the same as learning the intended knowledge and skills (Gilmour et al., 2019). In my opinion, schooling should place emphasis on students' learning the academic and self-help skills that are most important for the individual student's future. Learning is more important than just being there (in any particular place). Warnock (2005), once an advocate of the inclusion of all SEND in general education, noted how meaningful inclusion does not mean that all students must be, as she put it, "under the same roof." She understood that it is more important for SEND to be included in meaningful instructional activities than to be in the same place as children without disabilities.

Alas, some people still believe (and, perhaps, always will), in spite of all evidence and rational argument to the contrary, that the choice between appropriate instruction and the place of that instruction *never* is necessary. But Warnock's view, and all judgments about SEND (even their identification, if we are to have the category) requires us to draw lines, more specifically lines related to statistical distributions (Kauffman & Lloyd, in press). We must consider where the line is *best* drawn and then decide on which side of the line a given case falls. This is particularly difficult for cases in which an individual is on or close to the line. Drawing lines is absolutely unavoidable when the objective is to implement a program that benefits some but not all individuals or when the objective is to categorize or respond differently *in any way* to some individuals but not to others. That is, unless all individuals (or cases) are treated precisely the same, some criterion must be selected (i.e., a line must be drawn). Given a continuous distribution of the attribute involved, there will always be individuals on or near the line, regardless of whether the objective is to provide economic assistance or other help not available to all (Washington Post, 1996). This is merely the recognition of an artifact of measurement of continuous variables (Kahneman et al., 2021).

What teachers have to do is essentially the same as what is required in *any* profession or craft—draw lines and make judgments. The criteria for lines and judgments may be different, but lines must be drawn and the judgments must be made—e.g., for smoothness, sweetness, in-tuneness, brightness, net worth, learning, and so on. This kind of line-drawing and judgment-making is called discrimination—meaning noting a difference, not being unfair. It cannot be avoided even if all students with disabilities are to be included in general education—*if* we are to recognize SEND as a separate category or *if* we are to have educational tiers (Kauffman et al., 2022). Teachers' decisions involve uncertainty, and therefore error in judgment is inevitable (Kahneman, 2011; Kahneman et al., 2021).

One way to resolve this problem is eliminating judgment, just not having a category known as SEND and treating all students the same. Unfortunately, this eliminates only one problem, for teachers must make other judgments (e.g., what to teach to whom, which students have learned certain skills and which have not, what grade a student should be given) in which there is uncertainty (Kauffman et al., 2022).

Of course, there are those who argue for getting rid of all the uncertainty we can (e.g., grades, failure, categories, and names). If we have categories of any kind, then we are faced with the problem of communicating with others about them, and for this, we must have signals, usually words. So, unless we are to communicate with signs or vocalizations that are not words, we have to say the word. And, I might say in jest: "Oh, the horror!"

The problem

The problem is how and where to draw the line in any case, if choice is allowed. And this problem arises in all cases in which we allow choices or we have criteria for determining a particular category. A category has to have a name if we are to recognize its existence. Names are labels, and suggestions that we do away with labels are nonsensical if we are to take any action related to a category we believe exists (Kauffman, Anastasiou et al., 2024). Thus, people may be loath to acknowledge or create a category; then it is incumbent upon them to define its parameters. Defining the parameters of a category of disability is not typically an easy task, and interpreting or applying those parameters in individual cases is a fraught task for educators (Kauffman & Lloyd, in press). Of course, those who argue that drawing a line, particularly one defining SEND, prevents us from achieving social justice (e.g., Slee, 2018, 2019). They are likely to go on to argue that *all* children are different, *all* children are special in some way, *all* children should receive individualized attention to their educational needs, and in those ways, children with disabilities are not different from others. They are likely to argue that we cannot distinguish SEND from the general population of diverse children (e.g., Schifter & Hehir, 2018). They are likely to argue, for example, that we should have had an Education for All Children Act, that no classification of children should give them something essentially different from the education to which *all* children are entitled. There is a shard of truth in this contention, for disabilities are continuously distributed variables. Cut points that define categories are selected based on estimates of risk and benefit and can be changed at will. A reality is that some individuals will be near the chosen cut point and their status is therefore arguable (Kauffman & Lloyd, in press). The larger, more relevant, and more complete truth, however, is that without a line defining category X, we can provide no special services for those in category X. For example, if we want to provide economic assistance for people in the category "poor," then we must have a line or cut point regarding financial assets to create the category "poor" (Washington Post, 1996). Moreover, as Kauffman, Anastasiou et al. (2024) note, category X must have a name. Therefore, the argument that disability exists, although we have no line defining it or should not name it, is disingenuous, a gratuitous insult to SEND and a nullification of special education of any kind. It is much easier to assume that the category does not exist, to deny its reality, or insist that the category is mythical, existing only in the minds of the deluded. And, indeed, there are mythical categories of nearly every type, and some people are deluded. Myths and delusions are real categories for which we have names. Some myths are fantasies created for children's enjoyment. However, if myths are not made for anyone's entertainment, then they reveal a stunning naivete. Delusions can be part of mental illness, although they can also exist in the thought processes of those who have been fooled but are not diagnosed as having a mental illness. We might conclude that myths and delusions are real categories and that subcategories of them exist.

Drawing the line defining the category "mental retardation" or intellectual disability (ID, or intellectual and developmental disability, IDD) was highlighted by Dunn (1968) decades ago. The issues of lines defining all categories of disabilities are both essential and intractable—necessary but not solvable except by choices of criteria based on estimates of risks and benefits. Unsurprisingly, one response (popularized by DS and DSE) is denial that categories of disability exist, considering all disabilities to be normal variations or diversities. The consequences of this view are disastrous for the education of people with disabilities, with impairments that most of us believe are real, not social constructions (see Gordon Gould & Hornby, 2023; Hallahan, 2024; see also interview of Wolf Wolfensberger at youtube.com/watch?v=rKnZn0Ip4AM&ab_channel=InstituteonCommunityIntegration). Education, general and special, is beset by uncertainty, and although there may be ways to reduce it or increase it, uncertainty cannot be avoided (Kauffman, Badar et al., 2022).

Possible approaches to solving the problem

Holding onto the idea that "all means all," the inane idea that there are to be literally *no* exceptions to placement of SEND in general education, ignores the history and nature of human societies, the fate of past policies, and the way people become their own worst enemies (Kauffman, Anastasiou et al., 2020) see also interview of Wolfensberger). Defining exceptions, the criteria for creating a category or any kind related to education are problematic. Defining a category that is to be ignored, what Harden (2021) refers to as anti-classification, is relatively easy. For example, it is relatively easy to *prohibit* treating some categories, such as those defined by an individual's color, parentage, nation of origin, religion, or gender differently—and to do so in literally *all* cases. The category is recognized, but it is a category with no implications for education; therefore using it to make any educational decision is discriminatory. This approach—prohibition of treating individuals differently because of their categorization—to the education of SEND would be disastrous because classification as having a special educational need or disability would then be assumed to have no particular implications for education. Harden (2021) notes that the category of disability is different from other diversities in its implications for education and involves determination not to subordinate a classification of individuals. Anti-subordination is *not* prohibition of classification as a means of treating individuals unfairly but *required categorization with the intention of making education fairer*:

> The alternative to the "anti-classification" [e.g., *Brown v. Board of Education*, the 1954 U. S. Supreme Court decision prohibiting racial segregation in public education] approach to discrimination law is the "anti-subordination" approach, which focuses on raising the social status of certain marginalized or oppressed groups and preventing the formulation of an underclass. In contrast to anti-classification, which forbids differential treatment, anti-subordination allows for *positive* differential treatment. The Individuals with Disabilities Education Act (IDEA), for instance, takes an anti-subordination rather than an anti-classification approach. Under IDEA, children are held to have an equal right to a "free, appropriate public education." In designing an appropriate education, school systems are not only *allowed* to consider certain differentiating information about the individual student, they are, in fact, *mandated* to consider that information for accommodation and planning purposes.
>
> *(Harden, 2021, p. 245, italics in original)*

Making legal placement decisions under IDEA is difficult (Kauffman, Burke & Anastasiou, 2023). Not only is it difficult, but any choice from the continuum of alternative placements (CAP) demanded by the law (IDEA) is open to criticism and second-guessing. The alternative chosen from the CAP will be said by some *not* to be the least restrictive environment (LRE), another demand of the law. A dilemma inevitably accompanies classification in the anti-subordination approach: "*Damned if you do*" (+, assume that the category SEND implies need for a different education) and "*damned if you don't*" (−, do *not* assume that the category SEND implies need for a different education). Given this dilemma, it is easy to see why the anti-classification tactic is appealing, for it eliminates the + (i.e., the assumption that the SEND category implies the need for a different education) and, thereby, the dilemma. If the assumption is that we should not treat children in the category SEND differently from others, then we are relieved of some of the potential condemnation of our position. The only criticism, then, will come from those who oppose disregarding the difference as mandated in anti-classification. That is, the critics will be only those who, like me, believe that the difference must *not* be ignored and that special education like that prescribed by EAHCA/IDEA should be motivated by the anti-subordination idea.

Recognizing the implications of classification for a given activity is critical, and this is highlighted by concern for achieving diversity, equity, and inclusion (DEI) in a rational and legally tenable way. DEI can be rationally interpreted if the disability is seen as a particular kind of diversity that is perverted by anti-classification and requires judgment that most other diversities do not (Kauffman & Crockett, 2023; Kauffman, Polloway, & Hallahan, 2023). Failure to see how disability is not like other diversities for education is a failure of understanding that spells disaster for the education of SEND. Treating SEND like any other diversity trivializes the differences of these students, putting them on a par with diversities like skin color and other physical characteristics that have no implications whatever for education.

Make no mistake about this: I believe most individuals with disabilities have been horribly and unjustly treated, and that they are often discriminated against in a variety of ways and by thoughtless policies. All people need to recognize the abilities and values of people with disabilities. Nevertheless, one way of denying people with disabilities their full humanity and value is to maintain that there is nothing wrong with them, that their disabilities are not really impairments, that disability is chic or a positive characteristic, that disability is actually just a social construction meant to keep individuals with disabilities from being seen as equal to others without disabilities, that prevention of disability is misguided or evil, and so on. Not caring that people have disabilities is, I think, an atrocious insensitivity. In fact, I find the attitude that disabilities are just fine and we shouldn't care that people have them or try to prevent them an outrageous, stomach-turning brutality. I think we should care enough about people with disabilities to do what we can to help them cope with their limitations, achieve all they can, and live the happiest and most productive lives they can. Those are the things we hope for individuals without disabilities, and we would do well to wish them for everyone—literally.

Diversity and disability

Anti-special education, full inclusion advocates seem to think EAHCA/IDEA were/ are misguided and counterproductive (e.g., Cornett & Knackstedt, 2020; Schifter & Hehir, 2018; see also Kauffman, 1999–2000) because the law assumes that students with disabilities not only must be classified but treated differently because of that classification. The category of "students with special educational needs or disabilities" may well exist, they contend, but anti-classification arguments (like those in *Brown*) are sufficient, and anti-subordination legislation (like IDEA) only gives SEND a special *privilege* to which they are no more entitled than are *all* children. They are misclassified as members of a *special* category of pupils, and this "setting apart" of certain individuals is wicked and socially unjust. Lest readers think treating all diversities the same is an overblown notion of mine and deluded others, consider how disabilities have been lumped in with other categories of diversity. Consider this paragraph in which the author is insisting that "all means all:"

> The child who can't see, the child whose family has been displaced by war and don't speak the school's home language, the child who has difficulty with mobility, the child who doesn't hear, the child whose behaviour is very different or difficult, the child who will be absent for periods of time because of chronic illness or is from an itinerant family, or the child who can't communicate in the way that most other children do.
>
> *(Slee, 2018, p. 29)*

In Slee (2019), the following categories were said to be essentially the same, in that they are all to be included in general education: indigenous children, girls, children displaced by conflict or natural disasters, children who are minorities in ethnicity or religion, or tribe, impoverished children, traveler children, children with disabilities.

Lest readers think no one is actually spouting anti-special education rhetoric, consider not only Slee's writing but that some in DSE are said to be working against special education (e.g., Connor, 2014), that Connor (2020) has called special education "dangerous" (without defining the danger or weighing one danger against another) and that Baglieri et al. (2011) wrote, "what special education strives to enforce, DS seeks to dissolve" (p. 2130). Oliver (2000), a major figure in DS, said "I was and remain implacably opposed to the very existence of special education" (p. 6). Another wrote, "…inclusive education is a call for a reformulation of schooling wherein 'special' and 'regular' are jettisoned and the segregation of students with disabilities is seen as a relic of a bygone age" (Slee, 2018, p. 82). Hallahan (2024) and others in the special issue of *Exceptionality* edited by Burke et al. (2024) and Kauffman et al. (2023) have provided more detail of the anti-special education sentiment of what Fuchs and Fuchs (1994) called the full inclusion movement (FIM) decades ago. The FIM has flourished, not only in the USA but in publications of the United Nations, particularly its Convention on Rights of Persons with Disabilities (CRPD), which makes no mention of special education (Anastasiou et al., 2018) and Slee's (2019) "think piece," which equates disabilities with other diversities.

The FIM and flimflam

As Fuchs and Fuchs (1994) noted, the FIM is a radicalization of school reform that is contrary to Enlightenment thinking about evidence. It has also contributed to the "blurring" of differences between special and general education (Fuchs et al., 2010). The FIM has made placement, rather than instruction, the ostensible primary purpose of special education (Kauffman & Badar, 2014, 2016). It focuses more on the LRE (least restrictive environment) provision of the EAHCA/IDEA than its IEP (individual education program) mandate (Hallahan, 2024). One of its favored strategies has been the promotion of the multi-tiered system of supports (MTSS), a tactic that is increasingly popular but has little empirical support (Wiley & David, 2024; Wiley et al., 2022). As appears to be true for many or most (perhaps even all) social controversies, the arguments are asymmetrical—not balanced or matched in extremeness or completely the reverse of one another. In the case of inclusion, *all* is not argued against *none* but against many or most. No one I know of argues for full exclusion—that *no* SEND should be placed in general education, that *no* child with a disability should attend a general education class in the neighborhood school. I know of no one who is opposed to *all* inclusion. And no one I know of is willing to argue that SEND should *not* be given an appropriate education, so the issue comes down to how and where appropriate education is best achieved for the *individual* in the SEND category—*if* we are to have the category. U. S. law (and sound reasoning, as well) does not allow placement decisions to be made for groups or an entire category of children. The law governing special education is not anti-categorical. Some do, in fact, argue that appropriate education is (or could be) always best achieved in the general education environment (the GEE) and that the GEE can be reimagined or transformed such that it is appropriate and the best choice for *all* children (and no one I've heard of argues the opposite, that it can be made appropriate for *no* children with SEND).

The FIM has often been supported and sold to many—and sold with extraordinary guile. The nonsense is typically served up by very intelligent people who are leaders in special education and masters of misleading people with misrepresentations and lies. These misrepresentations and lies are repeated with such apparent sincerity and so often that the nonsense becomes accepted as truth (Fuchs et al., 2023; Gordon-Gould & Hornby, 2023; Hornby & Kauffman, 2023). The selling is abetted by those who know the falsehoods are for sale but choose to say nothing or defend the sale under the guise of freedom of speech. The similarity of this guilefulness in special education to political chicanery is disquieting. The argument eventually comes down to *all* v. *not all*. Those die-hard extremists who insist that all should be taken literally when we speak of placement, that *all means all* students should be in general education, that there is no nuance, no shade of meaning, no exception is breathtakingly disingenuous. Using the word "most" would leave the door open for alternative placements and avoid the policy trap described by Kauffman et al. (2020) and historic policy mistakes described by Kauffman et al. (2021). "Most" makes clear that in *most* cases students with SEND can and should be taught in general education classes, but it admits nuance, judgment, informed choice, not a doctrinaire, inflexible, dogmatic approach to placement that "all" implies.

"All means all" might be a sanctimonious resistance to the law, or it might be ignorance of the realities of teaching—or, perhaps both. Laski (1991, p. 412) wrote "All children with learning problems, whether they be "special education" students, "at-risk" students, or otherwise regarded as disadvantaged in schooling, belong in regular classroom environments." Taylor (1988, 2004) criticized the idea of the continuum (CAP) required by U.S. law as a trap in which those with disabilities become ensnared. Both are wrong. An argument frequently leveled against the view that a CAP is required is that general education must be "reimagined" so that it meets the educational needs of *all* children. Kauffman, Anastasiou et al. (2022) noted their agreement with Krauss (2012) that "A truly open mind means forcing our imaginations to conform to the evidence of reality, and not vice versa, whether or not we like the implication" (p. 140). So, what are the educational realities to which our imaginations must conform? This is a key question about many issues in education, and its answers certainly constrain efforts to reform education of any kind, general or special. In the case of special education it involves denials of realities like those such as those articulated by Taylor and Sailor (2024) and Taylor et al. (2024)

Educational realities

I need not belabor here either the lack of teachers or the lack of effective training. In short, those who believe that all teachers will be or can be properly trained to teach all students are living in a fantasy world. They seem to have no understanding of what most schools and their teachers are like, the problems they face, or the diversity of schools, teachers, and pupils in public education systems. They suppose that, unlike other professions and lines of work, special training for teaching students with disabilities is unnecessary because, they maintain, good teaching is good teaching regardless of the student. These same individuals may, however, think special training is important for teaching music, art, physical education, and for teaching certain topics such as science, math, or history at the secondary level.

In fact, nearly every profession and line of work recognizes the value of specialization. I and colleagues have noted the irrationality and devaluation of SEND or proposals that *all* students be taught in general education:

> A possible legacy of ... *habeas corpus* inclusion [is the presumption] that *all* public schools and *all* general education teachers recognize their responsibility and ability to teach *all* children regardless of any disability the student may have. ... In our estimation, it makes approximately the same degree of sense as the following:
>
> 1 All drivers will be licensed to drive all vehicles, with no special training or licensure to drive any trucks, buses, heavy equipment, or other vehicles not airborne.
> 2 All pilots will be expected to fly all airplanes for all purposes, regardless of the number or type of engine(s), size, or purpose.
> 3 All builders will be licensed to construct all types of buildings.
> 4 All physicians will be licensed to perform all medical treatments, including examinations, prescriptions, surgeries, and other medical procedures.
> 5 All hospitals will be open to all patients, and all patients will be placed in general medical units regardless of medical condition or diagnosis.
> 6 All soldiers will be expected to operate all weapons of defense and be trained to accomplish all missions.
> 7 All lawyers will be expected to handle all cases involving law, regardless of the nature of the case.
> 8 All teachers will be prepared to teach all subjects at all levels and to coach all sports.
> 9 All dentists will provide all dental services and procedures, including extractions, orthodontia, and dental implants.
>
> [T]he education endorsement that would be applied to all levels of instruction (K-12), all levels of severity, and all disability conditions. A similar proposal put forward for a single endorsement in general education that would qualify

an individual to teach anything from early childhood education to high school physics would be considered laughably outrageous! ... Such a proposal is not only unconscionable but reveals the devaluation of what special educators do and what students with disabilities deserve.

(Kauffman, Hallahan et al., 2020, pp. 257–259)

Robbins (2023) has realistically described how the inclusion of SEND in general education can work beautifully *sometimes, but not always*. Some children with SEND need a separate and special education (Gordon-Gould & Hornby, 2023). Moreover, not every teacher has the wherewithal to teach special education. Those who do have the wherewithal need recognition and support.

A reality that often gets overlooked is that we cannot improve the lives of school children without improving the lives of their teachers. Just as extraordinary claims require extraordinary evidence, extraordinary diversity of a group in knowing what is to be taught requires extraordinary skill in instruction. A reasonable question regarding teachers' work is how we might make it easier or harder. For any size of group, it is reasonable to assume that the greater the diversity of students (in knowledge and ability related to what is being taught, not other kinds of diversity), the harder the task of teaching. Yet, the notion of ability grouping is anathema to many educators. Some of the resistance to homogeneous grouping (homogeneous in the achievement of what is being taught) may be a result of science denial (Kauffman, 2011).

Another reality is that not all teachers (in fact, very few) are knowledgeable about every kind of disability and competent in teaching every skill. Few are polymaths. Like all of us, when asked to do things they cannot, teachers avoid the task; they bluff or simply resign.

The idea of equipping all teachers to teach all children may be pie-in-the-sky thinking, but the idea of having two teachers (one general, one special) in most, if not all, classrooms is no less a daydream, as this would require approximately doubling the number of teachers. The effect on education budgets would be enormous, not to mention problems in recruitment and training. The realities are that teacher training, compensation, and retention do not and are quite unlikely in the future to come anywhere near what would be required to implement full inclusion in a way that would benefit all or even most SEND. Proponents of full inclusion seem not to have thought through what taking their proposals to scale in a state or nation would require of teachers, teacher educators, or taxpayers. We do need to be open minded, in the sense of being willing to consider the alternative ways in which we can best accommodate the special needs of *individuals* with disabilities. As Krauss (2012) reminded us, we do not need to waste our time supposing that our imaginations need not be constrained by realities. Certainly, realities can be distasteful, but our distaste for reality does not give us a license to ignore it in imagining what is possible. Disabilities are realities we may find painful, but that is no reason to pretend they do not really exist or are social constructs, that impairments resulting from them are not real, or that we should not do what we can to amend them. Another reality about education involves economic differences among the families of SEND. The reality is that those with sufficient economic resources can always buy the education they want for their children. Hence, private schools not open to the funding and regulations/policies of those in the public sphere are an option for them. Those families of more modest means and the poor are not able to buy their way free of the vagaries of public school policies.

Conclusion

We ignore realities at our own peril. However, ignoring realities can also imperil the lives of others. Our ignoring climate change realities imperils the lives of all other human beings. Our ignoring of the realities of education and special educational needs imperils the lives of children, especially those with SEND.

The FIM has been the radicalization Fuchs and Fuchs (1994) described decades ago. It is supported by flimflam that denies realities (Fuchs et al., 2023; Gordon-Gould & Hornby, 2023; Hornby & Kauffman, 2023). It feeds on the denial of the brutal realities of disabilities and related educational impairments of children and youth. It depends on a literal interpretation of "all" that is inconsistent with reality.

References

Akst, D. (2022). *War by other means: How the pacifists of WWII changed America for good.* Melville House.
Anastasiou, D., Burke, M. D., Wiley, A. L., & Kauffman, J. M. (2024). The Telos of special education: A tripartite approach. *Exceptionality, 32*(2), 90–108.
Anastasiou, D., Gregory, M., & Kauffman, J. M. (2018). Commentary on Article 24 of the CRPD: The right to education. In *Commentary on the UN Convention on the Rights of Persons with Disabilities* (pp. 656–704). Oxford University Press.
Baglieri, S., Bejoian, L. M., Broderick, A. A., Connor, D. J., & Valle, J. (2011). [Re]claiming "inclusive education" toward cohesion in educational reform: Disability studies unravels the myth of the normal child. *Teachers College Record, 113*(10), 2122–2154.
Burke, M. D., Kauffman, J. M., & Wiley, A. L. (2024). Introduction to the special issue. *Exceptionality, 32*(2), 145–147.
Connor, D. J. (2014). The disability studies in education annual conference: Explorations of working within, and against, special education. *Disability Studies Quarterly, 34*(2) https://dsq-sds.org/index.php/dsq/article/view/4257
Connor, D. J. (2020). "I don't like to be told that I view a student with a deficit mindset": Why it matters that disability studies in education continues to grow. *Canadian Journal of Disability Studies.* Retrieved December 24, 2020 from https://cjds.uwaterloo.ca/index.php/cjds/article/view/689/936
Cornett, J., & Knackstedt, K. M. (2020). Original sin(s): Lessons from the US model of special education and opportunity for leaders. *Journal of Educational Administration, 58*(5), 507–530.
Dunn, L. M. (1968). Special education for the mildly retarded—Is much of it justifiable? *Exceptional Children, 35*(1), 5–22.

Fuchs, D., & Fuchs, L. S. (1994). Inclusive schools movement and the radicalization of special education reform. *Exceptional Children, 60*(4), 294–309.

Fuchs, D., Fuchs, L. S., & Stecker, P. M. (2010). The "blurring" of special education in a new continuum of general education placements and services. *Exceptional Children, 76*(3), 301–323. https://doi.org/10.1177/001440291007600304.

Fuchs, D., Mirowitz, H. C., & Gilbert, J. K. (2023). Exploring the truth of Michael Yudin's claim: The more time students with disabilities spend in general classrooms the better they do academically. *Journal of Disability Policy Studies, 33*(4), 236–252. http://dx.doi.org/10.1177/10442073221097713

Gilmour, A. F., Fuchs, D., & Wehby, J. H. (2019). Are students with disabilities accessing the curriculum? A meta-analysis of the reading achievement gap between students with and without disabilities. *Exceptional Children, 85*(3), 329–346.

Gordon-Gould, P., & Hornby, G. (2023). *Inclusion at the crossroads: Exploring effective special needs provision in global contexts*. Routledge.

Greenhouse, L. (2020, June 4). The Supreme Court, too, is on the brink. *New York Times*. https://www.nytimes.com/2020/06/04/opinion/supreme-court-religion-coronavirus.html?action=click&module=Opinion&pgtype=Homepage

Greenhouse, L. (2021). *Justice on the brink: The death of ruth bader ginsburg, the rise of Amy Coney Barrett, and twelve months that transformed the supreme court*. Random House.

Hallahan, D. P. (2024). Welcome to the destruction of special education in the name of ideology. *Exceptionality, 32*(2), 71–76.

Harden, K. P. (2021). *The genetic lottery: Why DNA matters for social equality*. Princeton University Press.

Hornby, G., & Kauffman, J. M. (2023). Special education's zombies and their consequences. *Support for Learning, 38*(3). https://doi.org/10.1111/1467-9604.12451

Kahneman, D. (2011). *Thinking, fast and slow*. Farrar, Straus and Giroux.

Kahneman, D., Sibony, O., & Sunstein, C. R. (2021). *Noise: A flaw in human judgment*. Little, Brown.

Kauffman, J. M. (1980). Where special education for disturbed children is going: A personal view. *Exceptional Children, 46*(7), 522–527.

Kauffman, J. M. (1989). The regular education initiative as Reagan-Bush education policy: A trickle-down theory of education of the hard-to-teach. *Journal of Special Education, 23*(3), 256–278. https://doi.org/10.1177/002246698902300303

Kauffman, J. M. (1999–2000). The special education story: Obituary, accident report, conversion experience, reincarnation, or none of the above? *Exceptionality, 8*(1), 61–71. https://doi.org/10.1207/S15327035EX0801_6

Kauffman, J. M. (2011). *Toward a science of education: The battle between rogue and real science*. Attainment.

Kauffman, J. M. (2015, September 15). Reflections on the life an works of Richard J. Whelan. Pdf available from author by request.

Kauffman, J. M. (2022). This one, not that one: Toward revitalizing special education. In J. M. Kauffman (Ed.), *Revitalizing special education: revolution, devolution, and evolution* (pp. 1–41). Emerald.

Kauffman, J. M., Ahrbeck, B., Anastasiou, D., Badar, J., Felder, M., & Hallenbeck, B. A. (2021). Special education policy prospects: Lessons from social policies past. *Exceptionality, 29*(1), 16–28. https://doi.org/10.1080/09362835.2020.1727326

Kauffman, J. M., Anastasiou, D., Badar, J., & Hallenbeck, B. A. (2020). Becoming your own worst enemy: Converging paths. In C. Boyle, J. Anderson, A. Page, & S. Mavropoulou (Eds.), *Inclusive education: Global issues & controversies*, Vol. 45. *Studies in inclusive education* (pp. 73–88). Brill Sense.

Kauffman, J. M., Anastasiou, D., Burke, M. D., Felder, M., Hornby, G., Lopes, J., & Wiley, A. (2024). Adventures in naming EBD realities: How words matter for special education. *Journal of Emotional and Behavioral Disorders, 32*(1), 3–13. https://doi.org/10.1177/10634266231172929

Kauffman, J. M., Anastasiou, D., Hornby, G., Lopes, J., Burke, M., Felder, M., Ahrbeck, B., & Wiley, A. (2022). Imagining and reimagining the future of special and inclusive education. *Education Sciences*. https://www.mdpi.com/2227-7102/12/12/903

Kauffman, J. M., & Badar, J. (2014). Instruction, not inclusion, should be the central issue in special education: An alternative view from the USA. *Journal of International Special Needs Education, 17*(1), 13–20. https://doi.org/10.9782/2159-4341-17.1.13

Kauffman, J. M., & Badar, J. (2016). It's instruction over place not the other way around! *Phi Delta Kappan, 98*(4), 55–59. https://doi.org/10.1177/0031721716681778.

Kauffman, J. M., & Badar, J. (2020). Definitions and other issues. In J. M. Kauffman (Ed.), *On educational inclusion: Meanings, history, issues and international perspectives* (pp. 1–24). Routledge.

Kauffman, J. M., Badar, J., Wiley, A. L., Anastasiou, D., & Koran, J. (2022). Uncertainty in education: Policy implications. *Journal of Education*. https://doi.org/10.1177/00220574221090283

Kauffman, J. M., Burke, M. D., & Anastasiou, D. (2023). Hard LRE choices in the era of inclusion: Rights and their implications. *Journal of Disability Policy Studies, 34*(1), 61–72. https://doi.org/10.1177/10442073221113074

Kauffman, J. M., & Crockett, J. B. (2023). DEI and its possible consequences for special education. Manuscript submitted for publication.

Kauffman, J. M., Hallahan, D. P., Landrum, T. J., & Smith, C. R. (2020). Likely legacies of inclusion. In J. M. Kauffman (Ed.), *On educational inclusion: Meanings, history, issues and international perspectives* (pp. 249–265). Routledge.

Kauffman, J. M., & Lloyd, J. W. (in press). Statistics, data, and special education decisions: Basic links to realities. In J. M. Kauffman, D. P. Hallahan, & P. C. Pullen (Eds.), *Handbook of special education* (3rd ed). Taylor & Francis.

Kauffman, J. M., Polloway, E. A., & Hallahan, D. P. (2023). The meaning of DEI for persons with IDD. *Global Journal of Intellectual & Developmental Disabilities, 12*(1). https://juniperpublishers.com/gjidd/pdf/GJIDD.MS.ID.555830.pdf

Krauss, L. A. (2012). *Universe from nothing: Why there is something rather than nothing.* Simon & Schuster.

Laski, F. J. (1991). Achieving integration during the second revolution. In Luanna. H. Meyer, Charles. A. Peck, & Lou. Brown (Eds.), *Critical issues in the lives of people with severe disabilities* (pp. 409–421). Paul H. Brookes.

Martin, E. W. Jr. (2013). *Breakthrough: Federal special education legislation 1965-1981.* Bardolf.

Oliver, M. (2000, July). *Decoupling education policy from the economy in late capitalist societies: Some implications for special education.* Keynote address at the International Special Education Congress, Manchester, England.

Orwell, G. (1954, original essay 1946). Politics and the English language. In *A collection of essays by George Orwell* (pp. 162–177). Doubleday Anchor.

Robbins, A. (2023). *The teachers: A year inside America's most vulnerable, important profession.* Dutton.

Schifter, L. A., & Hehir, T. (2018). The better question: How can we improve inclusive education? *Education Next, 18.* https://www.educationnext.org/better-question-how-can-we-improve-inclusion-education-response-has-inclusion-gone-too-far/#:~:text=Students%20can%20and%20should%20receive,to%20conflate%20placement%20with%20services.

Slee, R. (2018). *Inclusive education isn't dead, it just smells funny.* Routledge.

Slee, R. (2019). Defining the scope of inclusive education. *Think piece prepared for the 2020 Global Education Monitoring Report, Inclusion and Education.* United Nations Educational, Scientific and Cultural Organization.

Stainback, W., & Stainback, S. (1991). A rationale for integration and restructuring: A synopsis. In J. W. Lloyd, N. N. Singh, & A. C. Repp (Eds.), *The regular education initiative: Alternative perspectives on concepts, issues, and models* (pp. 226–239). Sycamore.

Stevens, S. (2023). *The conspiracy to end America: Five ways my old party is driving our democracy to autocracy*. Hachette.

Taylor, J. L., & Sailor, W. (2024). A case for systems change in special education. *Special and Remedial Education, 45*(2), 125–135.

Taylor, S. J. (1988). Caught in the continuum: A critical analysis of the principle of the least restrictive environment. *Journal of the Association for Persons with Severe Handicaps, 13*, 41–53.

Taylor, S. J. (2004). Caught in the continuum: A critical analysis of the principle of least restrictive environment. *Research and Practice for Persons with Severe Disabilities, 29*(4), 218–230. https://doi.org/10.2511/rpsd.29.4.218

Taylor, S. L., Proffit, F. W., Cornett, J., & Sailor, W. (2024). Unintended consequences of special education. *Journal of Special Education, 45*(2), 125–135.

Toobin, J. (2023). *Homegrown: Timothy McVeigh and the rise of right wing extremism*. Simon & Schuster.

Walker, H. M. (2003, February 20). *Comments on accepting the outstanding leadership award from the midwest symposium for leadership in behavior disorders*. Author.

Warnock, M. (2005). *Special educational needs: A new look. impact no. 11*. Philosophy of Education Society of Great Britain. https://www.researchgate.net/publication/330741940. Also available from author as pdf.

Washington Post (1996, November 24). Line drawing. C6.

Wiley, A. L., & David, D. (2024). Multi-tiered systems of support in special education reform: A critical appraisal. In J. M. Kauffman, D. P. Hallahan, & P. C. Pullen, *Handbook of special education* (3rd ed., pp. 23–38). Routledge.

Wiley, A. L., Harker, B., & McCollum, T. (2022). Veil of tiers or happy tiers? Revitalizing special education in an age of multi-tiered systems of support. In J. M. Kauffman (Ed.), *Revitalizing special education: Revolution, devolution, and evolution* (pp. 121–141). Emerald.

5

THEORISING THE INCLUSIONARY– EXCLUSIONARY CONTINUUM WHILE INVESTIGATING SCHOOL SITUATIONS

Johan Malmqvist

Introduction

This chapter begins with a brief description of the Swedish school context over the last three decades, particularly regarding compulsory education. This is followed by a detailed presentation of a theoretical model, *the Staircase Model of Inclusionary and Exclusionary Processes*, that the research team I lead is using in seven ongoing studies. The model was developed to serve as an analytical tool with which to gain insights into our collected data and to better understand the exclusionary development trajectory in Swedish schools. This is being done by investigating inclusionary and exclusionary processes, relating them forces inside and outside schools and to societal mechanisms underlying this trend.

The exclusionary development trajectory in Swedish schools

Since the 1990s, the Swedish school system has changed thoroughly, its governance is based on new public management (NPM), with an emphasis on "explicit standards and measures of performance; managing by results; value for money; and closeness to the customer" (Rhodes, 1996, p. 655). This has been combined with the introduction of incentive structures into public service, structures such as market competition, quasi-markets, and consumer choice (Rhodes, 1996). Many national reforms have also been implemented, such as decentralisation, the right to choose a school, and the establishment of independent schools (i.e. free schools) in a quasi-market developed for education. School companies are even allowed to make profits based on their tax-derived earnings (European Commission, 2022), without being required to invest these profits in schools, and this has attracted large

DOI: 10.4324/9781032705484-6
This chapter has been made available under a CC-BY 4.0 license.

limited liability companies (Alexiadou & Lundahl, 2019). No other country in the world allows this profit opportunity. Concurrently, since the early 1990s, segregation and inequity have increased in schools, while student academic achievement has deteriorated. Investigation was needed, so the first National School Commission (SOU, 2017, p. 35) since 1946 was created in 2015, and its main conclusion was that the Swedish school system has several serious systemic problems.

Another development that started in Sweden in the early 1990s has been the increasing frequency of ADHD diagnoses. Since then, there has been a dramatic increase in the number of students receiving medical diagnoses, especially of ADHD according to the National Board of Health and Welfare (Socialstyrelsen, 2023). Furthermore, Sweden has an extremely high proportion of students aged 5–19 years who receive medication for their ADHD, putting it in third place after the USA and Canada according to a recent study of 64 countries (Chan et al., 2023). Importantly, scholars have emphasised the connection between how schools function and the prevalence of ADHD diagnoses (Hinshaw & Scheffler, 2014).

Student misbehaviour and social order in schools are currently heavily debated in Sweden. The large proportion of students receiving diagnoses, for example, of ADHD, reveals the popularity of medical explanations and treatments to address these issues. The current Swedish national policy of increasing the number of special education classes, pupil referral units (PRUs), and emergency schools (Ministry of Education, 2023),[1] and thereby "fixing" students' "deficits" with exclusionary measures, seems to be the preferred way to address problems in the school system. Exclusionary measures are also increasingly being used for other student groups, as an increased number of students have been placed in schools for students with intellectual impairments (Skolverket, 2023a) and in special schools for students with physical impairments (Skolverket, 2023b). According to Gren Landell (2021), there are no official national data on attendance in Swedish schools; therefore, our knowledge about the problem of school absenteeism, particularly self-exclusion, is poor.

Paradoxically, the January Agreement[2] (Social Democratic Party, 2019) among the four political parties forming the government stated that inclusion had gone too far, but did not define what it meant by inclusion. This political agreement, which was a kind of statement of national policy, articulated nine broad goals in the educational sector. Goal 52 contains the specific sub-goals of enabling more special education classes and that PRUs should be made more available. The Agreement seemed to reflect a placement-based definition of inclusion corresponding to mainstreaming in schools rather than inclusive education (SOU, 2020, p. 42). The alternative to mainstreaming or exclusion, which would be to improve the schools' ability to offer inclusive education, was left out of the agreement.

Since my interview on the Inclusion Dialogue podcast in October 2021, when I expressed my concerns regarding this development trajectory in Sweden, the path away from inclusionary ambitions has become even more reified in a new party-political agreement (Tidö Agreement, 2022). This trajectory is not in accordance with the signing of the 2030 Agenda and its Sustainable Development Goals, particularly Goal 4 to "ensure inclusive and equitable quality education and promote lifelong learning opportunities for all" (United Nations, 2015). The present government seems to have prioritised homogeneous classes and counteracting disruptive behaviour in class. The main idea underlying these priorities seems to be the development of a school system better able to compete in OECD's PISA race.

This interesting exclusionary development trajectory in Swedish schools is currently being investigated by a research team I lead. The Swedish part of the team consists of ten colleagues from Linnaeus University, i.e. Tobias Björklund, Kristina Hellberg, Sofie Hammarqvist, Christina Linderos, Johanna Lüddeckens, Anette Mathisson, Corrado Matta, Henrik Nilsson, Josef Qaderi and Daniel Sundberg along with Gunvie Möllås from Jönköping University. Our international collaborators are Richard Rose of Northampton University and Michael Shevlin of Trinity College, University of Dublin. We have named our research programme Inclusive Research on Equity and Segregation in Schools (IRESS). It represents a shift away from our previous research interest in inclusion in Swedish schools and is informed by the large-scale project, Inclusive Research in Irish Schools (Rose et al., 2015). Now, we are focusing more on the opposite of inclusion: segregation and exclusion in Swedish schools.

A theoretical model with which to investigate inclusionary versus exclusionary development

This redirection of research focus called for a new theoretical framework, and work on a new model started in 2020. An early version, *The Segregation Staircase* theoretical model, was briefly described in the previously mentioned podcast. This model has been modified during our ongoing research work. Sofie Hammarqvist, a doctoral student, has made significant contributions to this model. We have recently renamed the model *The Staircase Model of Inclusionary and Exclusionary Processes* (Figure 5.1).

It should be noted that we are mainly conducting case studies in the current research programme. This is an advantage when it comes to theory development, according to Nilholm (2021), as case studies allow different levels to be analysed, from the classroom to system levels. Nilholm also emphasised the importance of longitudinal approaches. As our model focuses on processes, six of the seven studies include an attempt to collect longitudinal data by asking questions about interviewees' previous experiences. In one study, four students were followed over a three-year period. In three studies, school documentation has been collected and observations conducted in several different school settings. In three of the studies, in particular, rich mainly qualitative data have already been collected.

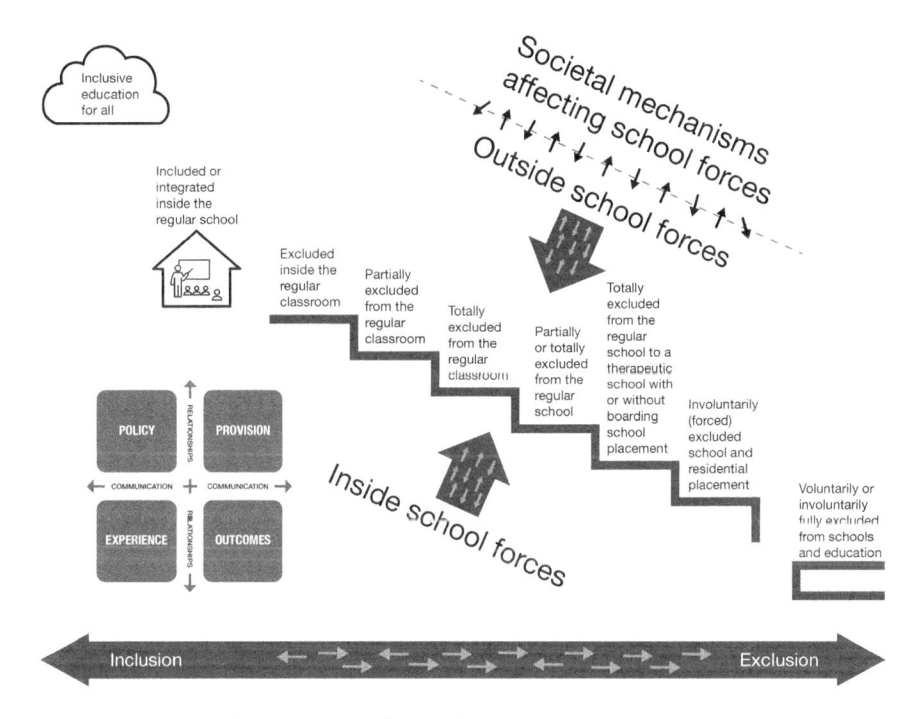

Theorising the Inclusionary–Exclusionary Continuum **65**

FIGURE 5.1   The Staircase Model of Inclusionary and Exclusionary Processes.

The staircase in the centre of the model

At the top of the staircase is a "cloud" representing a vision to strive for – "Inclusive education for all" – which corresponds to full inclusion. We view this as a vision, based on a definition of inclusion as containing all students, without any exclusion taking place. The centre of the model presents situations frequently encountered in most school systems and not specific to Sweden's. An image to the right of the cloud depicts a classroom situation in which students are "Included or integrated inside the regular school". This image of the classroom represents what we believe is possible in Sweden and other countries today. Note that the picture contains three students representing those who are largely included in the classroom situation, whereas the fourth represents a student in a mainstream or integrated[3] school situation.

It should also be noted that the model necessarily contains several simplifications. For example, when the four students continue to their next lesson, these four students' school situations may change. In another subject and perhaps under other conditions, such as having a different teacher who teaches in a different way, all four students may be included rather than being integrated, and feeling included, pointing to a contextual dimension. These four students' school situations may also change over time, pointing to a temporal dimension. Both these dimensions are present throughout the model, illustrating the importance of understanding processes rather than fixed states when trying to understand why schools are moving towards inclusive or exclusive education. Furthermore, inclusionary and exclusionary processes are occurring simultaneously in all schools, which means that both types of processes need to be investigated (Hedegaard Hansen, 2012). Such processes often lead to particular measures in school, which are focused on and described in the staircase model (Figure 5.1).

To the right of the classroom image is the "upper landing" of the staircase. It is the starting point of several exclusionary measures instituted as the staircase descends, resulting in increasingly exclusionary school situations. The first step is "Excluded inside the regular classroom", representing a school situation in which a student is excluded inside the classroom to some extent. Even though the student is physically present in the classroom, the degree of exclusion may be severe. This may be the case when, for example, a student is inside the classroom but is not allowed to participate in the same curricular activities as the other students or to interact socially with them. Specifically, the teacher may have stated that he/she does not want to teach this student, and the other students may socially exclude the student.

The next step down and to the right, "Partially excluded from the regular classroom", indicates a physical manifestation of exclusion, in which a student is not allowed to stay in the regular classroom during all lessons. Alternatively, the student is only given the opportunity for special needs support in a segregated setting, which leads to a similar segregated educational situation. For most students, this step is more exclusive than the previous step in the staircase. This may also be the case with the student in the example above whose excluded situation was severe inside the regular classroom. More precisely, that student may have a worse school situation if he/she is still being excluded in the classroom and an additional measure is to "push" the student out of the classroom for some lessons or activities during the week. However, this also depends on what kind of situation the student is being "pushed" into. Again, and as emphasised above, these examples indicate that the school situations in the staircase simplify conditions for certain students and that more dimensions must be incorporated to thoroughly understand a given school situation.

The main difference in the next step down the staircase, "Totally excluded from the regular classroom", is that that student is no longer part of education in the regular classroom. The student may still have relationships with students in the former class, meeting them on breaks and field days when there is no curricular content. The student may experience a totally excluded school situation alone with a teacher assistant or student assistant, or with a teacher in one-to-one teaching or in another group with other students who have left the regular classrooms. The students, however, still attend the regular school, but the quality of teaching as well as other dimensions of education may vary. Even if the teaching is of high quality and the social climate is good, the students are still part of an exclusionary situation as student placement is important in definitions of inclusion and exclusion (cf. Göransson & Nilholm, 2014).

The fourth step down towards more exclusion is "Partially or totally excluded from the regular school". This means that a student is placed in another school or school setting for several hours, subjects, or days every week for a period of weeks, months, or years, or even full time, with no planning for this student's return to the regular school setting. This type of school is often an organisational and educational solution when it has been established that the regular school cannot adequately address the student's needs, pedagogically or socially (Malmqvist, 2021). These schools may specialise in working with students perceived to have specific behavioural issues and/or specific diagnoses in which, for example, PRUs have specialised (Malmqvist, 2018; Malmqvist & Nilholm, 2016).

The next step is "Totally excluded from the regular school and sent to a therapeutic school, with or without boarding placement". In this penultimate step, with placement in a "therapeutic" school, the students are perceived to need psychological and/or medical treatment and/or to need a different social situation. Such school placement may include the student living in a boarding school arrangement.

In the last step of this staircase model, "Involuntarily (forced) excluded school and residential placement", students are subject to mandatory placement. In Sweden, these boarding schools, called residential homes, are governed by the Swedish National Board of Institutional Care (SiS). They provide individually tailored care, treatment, and education for young people perceived to have psychosocial problems, criminal behaviour, and substance abuse (or a combination). At some units, there are young people who have committed serious criminal offences. SiS's residential homes have the legal right to detain individuals by force.

Note that there are overlapping aspects among schools positioned on the three last steps. The use of psychological therapies, for example, may be common in schools on these three steps but are more frequently used in schools on the two lowest steps.

Intentionally, there is no lower landing in the staircase model. Below the staircase, to the right, are different groups of students who are no longer in education – as the label says: "Voluntarily or involuntarily fully excluded from schools and education". One group consists of young people who refuse to attend school; another group consists of young people who want to attend school but find it impossible. The reasons for self-exclusion may vary in both these groups. It should be noted that in Sweden, schools may only refuse to admit a student to school for a maximum of two periods/weeks a year, for a maximum of one week at a time. Home schooling is only permitted by Swedish legislation when teachers from a school visit a home to give lessons, as a support measure.

Interestingly, according to the same educational legislation, disciplinary measures partly overlap with measures for special needs support. For example, placement in a special class for a period is a disciplinary measure but is also described as a support measure. Such measures are sometimes described as forming a staircase of disciplinary measures based on educational legislation (Hulthén, 2014).

In sum, the theoretical model incorporates inclusive or integrated education for most Swedish students, some exclusionary measures, and even examples of "deep exclusion" when students refuse to attend school ("self-exclusion"). There is no indication of anything approaching the vision of "Inclusive education for all". This is no surprise, as the Swedish school system includes various types of schools for students with, for example, intellectual impairments or various disabilities (e.g. blindness, hearing impairments, and severe speech disorders). As the staircase model is poorly suited to these latter groups, we have also been working on parallel staircase models with steps differing from those in the above model. The model described here contains measures used in Sweden to address behavioural issues.

Characteristics of the staircase model and its central parts

The idea of describing a certain order of different types of schools, as in the above model, is not new. In his pyramidal model, which he called "a hierarchy", Reynold (1962) focused on ten types of school situations within special education for handicapped children.

Our idea with this theoretical model is to go further than just presenting different school situations in a certain order, as in Reynold's model. It represents an attempt to better understand processes, conditions, measures, forces, and mechanisms, which are categories we have found to be workable and informative. The model's simplification of the reality in schools is based on our present understanding, which obviously corresponds to our assumptions about how things work regarding inclusionary and exclusionary processes along the staircase. The model presented here is not meant to be the final version, but remains in ongoing development. The model builds to a large extent on other researchers' work and is informed by their proposed theoretical contributions. These are described under five headings:

- A dynamic continuum understanding of inclusion and exclusion
- Understanding the dynamics (with the subheadings "Inside school forces" and "Outside school forces")
- Societal mechanisms affecting the school forces
- Policy–provision–experiences–outcomes
- Transactional theory

A dynamic continuum understanding of inclusion and exclusion

In a review, Göransson and Nilholm (2014) investigated various definitions of inclusion used in research, but all their reported definitions seemed to represent a static understanding. We have instead been inspired by Hedegaard Hansen (2012), who stated that "we cannot investigate inclusion without investigating exclusion" (p. 89). Our main interest, considering the situation in Sweden, is in understanding the development trajectory in schools, but not with inclusion as the main focus. An analytical "flip-flop" strategy was used in which "one looks at an opposite or extreme range of a concept to bring out its significant properties" (Corbin & Strauss, 2008, p. 16). Consequently, the focus was directed towards the opposite of what the concept of inclusion stands for, and we ended up investigating exclusion. As the large arrow at the bottom of the model shows, our main interest in investigating exclusionary processes also encompasses an interest in inclusionary processes (Figure 5.1). We understand these processes as always being present along a continuum with two endpoints: full inclusion and, what has been termed "deep exclusion" by Daniels and Cole (2010). Intentionally, within the large, dark arrow at the bottom of Figure 5.1, more smaller arrows are pointing towards exclusion rather than to inclusion. This is in accordance with how we view the present development trajectory in the Swedish school system.

Understanding the dynamics

We need to understand the forces underlying exclusionary processes. In endeavouring to do so, we are especially focusing on students' experiences along the continuum, as well as on their legal guardians' perspectives. Our studies are accordingly designed to provide empirical findings, especially related to inside school forces, as they are understood by students and their legal guardians, as well as by school staff. At the same time, we will to some extent be able to refer to external school forces and, at a theoretical level, to the mechanisms underlying such internal and external school forces. To do this, we apply transactional theory.

Inside school forces

The "push" factor in the push–pull factor theory (Myklebust, 2002) has been used to better understand what students experience in their school situations and when moving along the staircase as well as how schools handle students considered challenging. According to Myklebust (2002), the theory has been used in educational research, for example, regarding the transitional patterns of groups of special-needs students during their time in school. It has also been used in studies of early school leavers (Nikou & Luukkonen, 2024). Nes et al. (2018) used the terms "pull out" and "push out" to refer to all forms of classroom leaving, especially when students leave the regular classroom and learn in settings separated from their peers.

In our studies, we have used the term "push-out factors" to refer to forces that appear to contribute to social, educational, and physical exclusion inside or outside a classroom or school. We have found several push-out factors, such as teachers who do not want to have certain students in their classrooms or students who are bullied by other students and, consequently, do not want to attend school. We have also found factors that seem to counteract such push-out factors, for example, teachers who socially and educationally provide the same students with a supportive learning environment where they can thrive. We call these "stay-in factors" (cf. Demo et al., 2023).

Outside school forces

In our model, outside school forces refer to forces outside the school contributing to students leaving their classrooms and/or schools. In our studies exploring pull-out factors related to outside school forces, we have found examples such as local teachers' union actions encouraging schoolteachers to report school incidents to the police (cf. Allan, 2006). Although such incidents may involve only very young children in their early school years, they may make other teachers reluctant to teach these young children. Another example is parent groups that demand that the school move a student or students of middle school away from the school; these young students are only 10–12 years old.

Societal mechanisms affecting school forces

Underlying the inside and outside school forces in our model are what we call societal mechanisms. One such mechanism is the governance of schools by educational legislation that may be more inclined towards inclusion or exclusion.

The following example is based on a School Commission report (SOU, 2020, p. 42) in which one municipality is regarded as a stakeholder. Several stakeholders were involved, one being the Swedish Association of Local Authorities and Regions, which supported the municipality. In 2014, the School Inspectorate decided that the municipality was contravening educational legislation with their PRUs. The municipality objected, arguing that as independent schools had the legal right to administer PRUs for students with special needs, diagnoses, or disabilities, municipalities should be able to compete with the companies that administer independent schools specialising in students needing special support. In 2017, the Supreme Administrative Court established that municipally run PRUs are legal, which led to a national increase in the number of PRUs, a development not aligned with the policy of the 2014–2018 government. This may also be viewed as an example of understanding governance according to governance network theory, in which one municipality and the Swedish Association of Local Authorities and Regions, as stakeholders, were influential when they opposed the national policy (Ansell et al., 2023).

Policy–provision–experiences–outcomes

In the bottom left-hand corner of Figure 5.1 is a model developed in Project IRIS (Rose et al., 2015) to assess progress towards inclusive education in Ireland. At the core of this model are four interrelated components seen as critical for developing the effective delivery of a more equitable and inclusive education system. These four components – policy, provision, experiences, and outcomes – were seen to affect the ability of schools and other agencies in their efforts to become more inclusive. Each component can be identified as affecting the steps of the staircase model presented here when school situations and transitions between them are investigated. This model is used to advance our knowledge of transitions in both exclusionary and inclusionary directions.

Transactional theory

Our understanding of processes is based on transactional developmental theory (Sameroff & Fiese, 2008), which is indicated in Figure 5.1 by the small arrows pointing in opposite directions inside the two arrows representing the inside and outside school forces and on the demarcation line separating the societal mechanisms from the school forces. Transactional theory, originating from developmental psychology focusing on child development, has also been used to understand interactional processes and the development of societal systems (Lorion, 2011) and seems to be compatible with governance network theory (Ansell et al., 2023). The development trajectory of schools, and of the school system as we understand it, seems to be dependent on negotiations at several societal levels from the classroom to the government. There also seem to be multiple alliances among stakeholders, such as researchers, interest groups, the teachers' union, national school authorities, school companies, and municipalities. We have found that even small Facebook groups can affect decision-making by national school authorities. For example, a Facebook group[4] of legal guardians strongly criticised the National Agency for Education's in-service teacher training in 2018. In conjunction with a public debate in one of Sweden's national daily newspapers,[5] there was a parallel debate in social media. The representatives of the Facebook group were eventually invited to a dialogue, which later led to changes in the in-service training regarding what teachers should know about neuropsychiatric diagnoses.[6] Before these changes, the government listened to the Facebook group, and the National Agency of Education was required by the government to participate in a dialogue with the group. The Facebook group's homepage contains many posts strongly criticising inclusion, claiming that the Swedish National Agency for Education lacks scientific competence regarding neuropsychiatric diagnoses. Hence, the top-down straightforward steering from the government via the national school authorities to the classroom does not seem to be the only direction of influence. Rather, there seems to be bidirectional influence with a dynamic in which many stakeholders participate in a process that fosters multiple changes over time. This example – one of many – reflects developmental changes in which a transactional understanding seems to be a valuable part of the analysis of the development trajectory in schools.

Concluding thoughts

The development trajectory in Swedish schools has raised concerns among many educational researchers in the country. The movement towards inclusive education seems to have weakened, while the movement towards exclusion in the school system seems to be growing stronger. This is a development that should be worrying for the Swedish government as well. Sweden has, as previously mentioned, agreed to work towards inclusive education (United Nations, 2015). Sweden is also a Member State in the Council of Europe, an organisation that, in a position paper, has declared segregation to be

> ... one of the worst forms of discrimination and a serious violation of the rights of the children concerned, as their learning opportunities are seriously harmed by isolation and lack of inclusion in mainstream schools.
> *(Council of Europe, 2017, p. 5)*

The described development trajectory is probably not unique to Sweden, as we are living in a globalised world where many societal trends have become common in many countries. For example, NPM is a strong movement in many countries, and there has been a worldwide trend towards the increased medicalisation of young students' behaviour. However, it is difficult to determine whether there has been a similar trend towards exclusion in other countries. Organisations such as the European Agency for Special Needs and Inclusive Education (EASIE) report on developments in their member countries. According to EASIE's most recent report (EASIE, 2024), several of its 31 member countries offer inclusive education to nearly 100 per cent of their school students, whereas Sweden is in last place regarding such education for students at both the primary and lower secondary school levels. This may be interpreted as indicating that the trend towards exclusion in schools is particularly characteristic of Sweden. As every country uses its own definition of inclusive education, however, comparisons across countries are difficult to make and potentially misleading. In England, for example, which according to the reported data has a much higher proportion of students in inclusive education than does Sweden, recent reports have shown an ongoing increase in suspensions and permanent exclusions from school (Department for Education, 2023). This background calls for research investigating not only the present state of inclusion and exclusion in schools, but also the development trajectory, when appropriate theoretical tools are available. As development is based on processes, research based on a static idea of inclusive education seems unproductive. Additionally, controversies over definitions of what constitutes inclusive education are based on static ideas that seem to lead only to dug-in stakeholder positions, but "it seems feasible to reach agreement about what (e.g. attitudes) is in favour of and what is against inclusion" (Malmqvist, 2016).

To summarise and conclude this chapter, in Sweden, and probably in other countries, there is an urgent need to better understand the trend towards exclusion in school systems and the processes that lead towards inclusion versus exclusion. Understanding these processes calls for a better understanding of the forces inside and outside schools that have influenced these processes and how they function.

These processes are affected and steered by a number of societal mechanisms. *The Staircase Model of Inclusionary and Exclusionary Processes* has been developed to provide researchers with a theoretical tool for more thoroughly understanding developments favouring inclusion versus exclusion in schools. The findings from a retroductive study (Malmqvist, 2016), mentioned in the *Inclusion Dialogue* podcast in October 2021, indicate that educational quality in addressing behavioural issues is crucial for students at risk for exclusion. We hope that research based on this model, which fosters a deeper understanding of inclusionary and exclusionary processes in schools, will also lead to actions that benefit students, particularly those who need high-quality educational support.

Notes

1 Placement in an emergency school is a time-restricted (four weeks) measure when disciplinary measures such as placement in a special class within a regular school have not worked. https://www.skolverket.se/skolutveckling/inspiration-och-stod-i-arbetet/stod-i-arbetet/starta-och-bedriva-akutskola
2 The election in September 2018 ushered in a period of no national government. The January Agreement, reached in January 2019, was a political pact among four political parties to establish a new Swedish government; the Agreement ended during a governmental crisis in 2021.
3 In Sweden, the word "integration" is used to describe mainstreaming based on the Latin root "bring parts together", i.e., segregation is not a precondition for this.
4 https://www.facebook.com/barnibehov
5 *Svenska Dagbladet* (a Swedish daily newspaper): debate articles from 2018-01-01 (https://www.svd.se/a/p6p6dE/skolverket-blundar-for-det-vi-vet-om-npf) to 2021-03-01 (https://www.svd.se/a/yRmvEx/skolverket-dribblar-bort-fragan-om-npf).
6 The term "*neuropsykiatriska funktionsnedsättningar*" (neuropsychiatric disabilities) is widely used in Sweden instead of the correct translation of "neurodevelopmental disorders" from DSM5.

References

Alexiadou, N., & Lundahl, L. (2019). The boundaries of policy learning and the role of ideas: Sweden, as a reluctant policy learner? In U. Stadler-Altmann & B. Gross (Eds.), *Beyond erziehungswissenschaftlicher grenzen: Diskurse zu entgrenzungen der disziplin* (pp. 63–77). Berliner Wissenschafts-Verlag GmbH.
Allan, J. (2006). The repetition of exclusion. *International Journal of Inclusive Education, 10*(2–3), 121–133. https://doi.org/10.1080/13603110500221511
Ansell, C., Sørensen, E., & Torfing, J. (2023). Public administration and politics meet turbulence: The search for robust governance responses. *Public Administration, 101*(1), 3–22. https://doi.org/10.1111/padm.12874
Chan, A. Y. L., Ma, T.-T., Lau, W. C. Y., Ip, P., Coghill, D., Gao, L., Jani, Y. H., Hsia, Y., Wei, L., Taxis, K., Simonoff, E., Taylor, D., Lum, T. Y., Man, K. K. C., & Wong, I. C. K. (2023). Attention-deficit/hyperactivity disorder medication consumption in 64 countries and regions from 2015 to 2019: A longitudinal study, *eClinicalMedicine, 58*, 101780, https://doi.org/10.1016/j.eclinm.2022.101780
Corbin, J., & Strauss, A. (2008). *Basics of qualitative research: Techniques and procedures for developing grounded theory* (3rd ed.). SAGE. https://doi.org/10.4135/9781452230153

Council of Europe (2017). *Fighting school segregation in Europe through inclusive education: A position paper.* The Council of Europe, Commissioner for Human Rights.

Daniels, H., & Cole, T. (2010). Exclusion from school: Short-term setback or a long term of difficulties? *European Journal of Special Needs Education, 25*(2), 115–130. https://doi.org/10.1080/08856251003658652

Demo, H., Nes, K., Somby, H. M., Frizzarin, A., & Zovo, S. D. (2023). In and out of class – What is the meaning for inclusive schools? Teachers' opinions on push-and pull-out in Italy and Norway. *International Journal of Inclusive Education, 27*(14), 1592–1610. https://doi.org/10.1080/13603116.2021.1904017

Department for Education (2023). *Suspension and permanent exclusions in England* [online]. GOV.UK. https://explore-education-statistics.service.gov.uk/find-statistics/suspensions-and-permanent-exclusions-in-england/2022-23-autumn-term

European Agency for Special Needs and Inclusive Education (2024). In P. Drál, A. Lenárt and A. Lecehval (Eds.), *European Agency Statistics on Inclusive Education: 2020/2021 school year dataset cross-country report.* Odense: EASNIE.

European Commission, Directorate-General for Education, Youth, Sport, & Culture (2022). *Education and training monitor 2022: Sweden.* Publications Office of the European Union. https://doi.org/10.2766/80995

Göransson, K., & Nilholm, C. (2014). Conceptual diversities and empirical shortcomings: A critical analysis of research on inclusive education. *European Journal of Special Education, 29*(3), 265–280.

Gren Landell, M. (2021). Introduction. In M. Gren Landell (Ed.), *School attendance problems: A research update and where to go* (pp. 19–38). Jerringfonden.

Hedegaard Hansen, J. (2012). Limits to inclusion. *International Journal of Inclusive Education, 16*(1), 89–98. https://doi.org/10.1080/13603111003671632

Hinshaw, S., & Scheffler, R. (2014). *The ADHD explosion: Myths, medication, money and today's push for performance.* Oxford University Press.

Hulthén, E.-L. (2014). Upptrappade åtgärder mot stök i skolan. [Escalated measures against disruptions in school]. *Pedagogiska Magasinet, 19*(2).

Lorion, R. P. (2011). Understanding Sarason's concepts of school cultures and change: Joining a community in school improvement efforts. *American Journal of Community Psychology, 48*(3–4), 147–156.

Malmqvist, J. (2016). Working successfully towards inclusion—or excluding pupils? A comparative retroductive study of three similar schools in their work with EBD. *Emotional and Behavioral Difficulties, 21*(4), 344–360. https://doi.org/10.1080/13632752.2016.1201637

Malmqvist, J. (2018). Has schooling of ADHD students reached a crossroads? *Emotional and Behavioural Difficulties, 23*(4), 389–409. https://doi.org/10.1080/13632752.2018.1462974

Malmqvist, J. (2021). The PRU: The solution for whom? *Education Sciences, 11*(9), 545. https://doi.org/10.3390/educsci11090545

Malmqvist, J., & Nilholm, C. (2016). The antithesis of inclusion? The emergence and functioning of ADHD special education classes in the Swedish school system. *Emotional and Behavioural Difficulties, 21*(3), 287–300 https://doi.org/10.1080/13632752.2016.1165978

Ministry of Education (2023). Förordning (2023:117) om statsbidrag för personalkostnader för akutskolor, speciallärare och elevhälsan [Regulation (2023:117) on state subsidies for personnel costs for emergency schools, special education teachers, and student health]. Ministry of Education. https://www.riksdagen.se/sv/dokument-och-lagar/dokument/svensk-forfattningssamling/forordning-2023117-om-statsbidrag-for_sfs-2023-117/

Myklebust, J. O. (2002). Inclusion or exclusion? Transitions among special needs students in upper secondary education in Norway. *European Journal of Special Needs Education, 17*(3), 251–263. https://doi.org/10.1080/08856250210162158

Nes, K., Demo, H., & Ianes, D. (2018). Inclusion at risk? Push- and pull-out phenomena in inclusive school systems: The Italian and Norwegian experiences. *International Journal of Inclusive Education*, *22*(2), 111–129. https://doi.org/10.1080/13603116.2017.1362045

Nikou, S., & Luukkonen, M. (2024). The push-pull factor model and its implications for the retention of international students in the host country. *Higher Education, Skills and Work-Based Learning*, *14*(1), 76–94. https://doi.org/10.1108/HESWBL-04-2023-0084

Nilholm, C. (2021). Research about inclusive education in 2020: How can we improve our theories in order to change practice? *European Journal of Special Needs Education*, *36*(3), 358–370. https://doi.org/10.1080/08856257.2020.1754547

Reynold, M. D. (1962). A framework for considering some issues in special education. *Exceptional Children*, *28*(7), 367–370.

Rhodes, R. A. W. (1996). The new governance: Governing without government. *Political Studies*, *4*(4), 652–667. https://doi.org/10.1111/j.1467-9248.1996.tb01747.x

Rose, R., Shevlin, M., Winter, E., & O'Raw, P. (2015). *Project IRIS. Inclusive research in Irish schools* (National Council for Special Education Research Report 20). NCSE.

Sameroff, A. J., & Fiese, B. H. (2008). Transactional regulation: The developmental ecology of early intervention. In J. P. Shonkoff & S. J. Meisels (Eds.), *Handbook of early childhood intervention* (pp. 135–159). Cambridge University Press. https://doi.org/10.1017/CBO9780511529320.009

Skolverket [Swedish National Agency for Education] (2023a). *Elever i grundsärskolan: Läsåret 2022/23* [Students in compulsory school for pupils with learning disabilities: Academic year 2022/23].

Skolverket [Swedish National Agency for Education] (2023b). *Elever i specialskolan: Läsåret 2022/23* [Students in special schools: Academic year 2022/23].

Social Democratic Party (2019). *January Agreement*. https://www.socialdemokraterna.se/download/18.1f5c787116e356cdd25a4c/1573213453963/Januariavtalet.pdf

Socialstyrelsen. [National Board of Health and Welfare] (2023). *Diagnostik och läkemedelsbehandling vid adhd. Förekomst, trend och könsskillnader.* [*Diagnostics and Pharmacological Treatment of ADHD. Prevalence, Trends, and Gender Differences.*]

SOU 2017:35 [Swedish Government Official Reports 2017:35] (2017). *Samling för skolan: Nationell strategi för kunskap och likvärdighet: Utbildningsdepartementet* [Gathering for school: National strategy for knowledge and equity]. Ministry of Education. https://www.regeringen.se/contentassets/e94a1c61289142bfbcfdf54a44377507/samling-for-skolan—nationell-strategi-for-kunskap-och-likvardighet-sou-201735.pdf

SOU 2020:42 [Swedish Government Official Reports 2020:42] (2020). *En annan möjlighet till särskilt stöd: Reglering av kommunala resurskolor* [Another special provision alternative: Regulation of municipal pupil referral units]. Ministry of Education. https://www.regeringen.se/49ec22/contentassets/0966298832c643809905412ddc67414a/en-annan-mojlighet-till-sarskilt-stod–reglering-av-kommunala-resursskolor-sou-202042

Tidö Agreement (2022). *Agreement for Sweden: The Tidö Agreement.* https://via.tt.se/data/attachments/00551/04f31218-dccc-4e58-a129-09952cae07e7.pdf

United Nations (2015). *The 2030 agenda for sustainable development.* https://sdgs.un.org/2030agenda

6
CONTEMPORARY COMPLEXITIES OF INCLUSIVE EDUCATION IN THE UNITED STATES

Amanda Miller and Susan Gabel

Introduction

This chapter stems from an interview with Dr Joanne Banks on her Inclusion Dialogue podcast in September 2021. Most of the conversation has not been modified; only minor grammatical edits have been made. In this conversation, Drs. Susan Gabel and Amanda Miller describe how discourses, ideologies, policies, and practices focused on disability have changed and/or not since their early experiences as general education and special education teachers/inclusion facilitators. This dialogue includes the following key topics: early career experiences in education, language, and context complexities, changes over time, contemporary critical, intersectional special education research with youth, federal legislation misinterpretation and lack of accountability, and state policy influences on preparation programs. While these were key points at the time of the exchange in September 2021, the legacy of these concerns persists. Gabel and Miller emphasize recent scholarship grounded in the creative acts of resistance and generative ideas girls of color with complex support needs bring forth. Finally, they also discuss youth-led and family-centered solutions for more authentically equitable and just schooling.

Early career experiences in the United States (US)

Joanne: Do you mind if I ask how you're working in this field? What brought you to work within this area of inclusive education?

Susan: Well, I have to go back to 1975. In the US, which is the year that our first federal legislation was approved for special education, I was in college at the time trying to choose a major and I chose special education. So, from there, I became a teacher. Early in my teaching career,

Contemporary Complexities of Inclusive Education **77**

I became a mother. Let's see, my second job in teaching was in a school for what they called at the time the neurologically impaired. This was in 1980. And I became a mother, through my teaching. My oldest son now at the time was my student. And he on the first day, he came to school, walked up to me looked up at me, he was very, very young, I was teaching the young children. And he said, "Mommy." From then on, I've been involved very deeply as a special ed mother, as a special ed teacher and now as a special education professor.

Joanne: I'm really interested in hearing your views on how you even mentioned language there, and how we titled things, but how that's changed over time. But before I before I come back to you on that, Amanda, I'd love to hear the same about how you're working in special education. What brought you here?

Amanda: Thanks for having us, I appreciate it. I think it's a little hard for me to answer that question because I feel like inclusive education is education (and whatever we are doing right now is not education). I was originally a general education teacher or initially a general education teacher. Before that, I was a substitute teacher and experienced subbing in classrooms that were segregated, and then when I had my own classroom, some of my students were being pulled out for services. And I was just really grappling with, like, why I couldn't teach them in our class, or why their teacher couldn't come into our class or like, how collaboration could look. So, then it was after that, that I pursued my master's in inclusive education for youth with more complex support needs. I've always been really interested, or intrigued by how people with disabilities are treated from an early age; like within my family, my cousin, my sister, even myself; like how difference was perceived and positioned by relatives. And so just seeing those connections, then within school, and what that meant with how children were thought of as learners or not was really important for me to uncover more deeply.

Language complexities, contexts, and change over time

Joanne: And if I could put the question to the two of you then as to change over time because you mentioned the 70s and the 80s. And certainly, from an Irish perspective, it's a bit harsh to talk about that now because language changes, attitudes change. Has that change happened in the U.S.?

Susan: I think it has. In some ways, it hasn't in some ways. I remember being a college senior I think, and I went to a conference hosted by the Council for Exceptional Children, which we still have in America. And the term that was used for students with disabilities was exceptional. That was the way we set it so that it was comfortable for everyone, right. And now, people are still using that term. But a new term more frequently used is special, they're special. So, language has changed, but remnants of this old language remain. And because language has changed and hasn't changed, new practices and policies have also emerged, but we've also kept qualities of previous practices and policies.

Joanne: Yeah. Amanda, if I could put it to you. I mean, Ireland at the moment is, over the last decade, like we've begun to open up more special education sessions for children and young people in the form of what we call special classes that are located within mainstream schools. For listeners that aren't familiar with the US context, if a student has a disability, I know this might vary by kind of category of disability, if you like, what's, what's available to them? Is it special education settings, withdrawal, special schools, like what what's available for students and their families?

Amanda: You're right, it does depend on disability label and local context. But really, all of those are available, including charter schools, public schools that are more inclusive, public schools that are more segregated. So special education classrooms, within the school, all the way to segregated schools, special schools, and depending on what state you live in they're called different names.

Susan: I can remember back in the 70s and early 80s, the kind of child who would be identified for special ed and then sent to a special education context. Typically, they were always segregated contexts, usually special schools, very rarely in the regular school. And many of those children who in those days would be sent to a special school are now in our regular schools, possibly even in the regular classroom much of the day. So that has changed a lot over the years for some groups of kids, particularly students with learning disabilities or speech and language impairments. But students with cognitive impairments, which is what Michigan calls intellectual disability, and severely multiple impaired students here in Michigan they tend to be in very segregated settings.

Contemporary critical, intersectional special education research

Joanne: And we'll be similar enough here. Can I bring you up to the present day now and just ask you to talk a little bit about your own research and what you are passionate about in this area, and maybe highlight some of the key tensions that exist today?

Susan: I think Amanda should be here. She's very actively researching.

Amanda: Well, I think before I begin, I did want to mention that the conversation, I think that we could have an entire well maybe already have an entire podcast on the conversation around language. It is so dynamic and informs how we think and what we do. Yeah, so anyways, um, so I have three lines of inquiry. The one I wanted to talk about today focuses on youth perspectives. I think that youth have so many important ways of looking

	at life, problem solving, solution generating. But we often discount their perspectives and experiences claiming they're too young or they don't know or they're going to ask for too much. And so, these perspectives are often left out of research. So that's my main line of inquiry, I could say, is youth perspectives and I focus on the perspectives of girls of color with particular disability labels, including autism, intellectual disability, and multiple disabilities as well as girls of color without disability labels, but primarily disabled girls of color in middle school and high school. And that was my dissertation research. Right now, I'm working on a local project here in Detroit, that is a youth-led project led by two Black girls in high school. I think it's asset and strengths based to learn from youth; there's just so much that we can uncover. They don't ask for too much. They're just asking for the basics and they're often not getting them.
Joanne:	What are your findings?
Amanda:	Sure. So, from my dissertation research, the participants, 9 disabled girls of color in middle school and high school, really wanted to take general education classes, almost all of them really wanted to take general education classes. But most of them either could not or were only allowed to take what we call like Specials or Electives here in the US like art, physical education, choir. But they wanted to take math, language arts, social studies, science. They were often really segregated. The learning in their classrooms was really missing so much meaningfulness. It just wasn't a rich learning environment, they often didn't have access to the same learning materials and tools as their peers, whether it be math manipulatives, different science, learning tools, all the way to access to iPads and laptops, even writing tools, they didn't necessarily have a choice about what they wrote with (Miller & Kurth, 2022).
Joanne:	So, did they comment at all about the expectations of staff, teachers, or leaders or even their parents did that come up?
Amanda:	I mean, a lot of their parents were really advocating for richer learning environments but weren't being heard. The girls had a ton of solutions, including access to libraries and books wherein they were represented, you know? Like, where there was representation of culture and language and experience. So, they definitely exposed a lot of gaps (Miller, 2023, 2024a).
Joanne:	I asked then, did you get anywhere with kind of the outcomes for students in those settings, so their transitions out of special education and into adult life? I know in the Irish context we don't have a lot of literature around racial differences in their experiences of education. But we possibly do so more in terms of socioeconomic, kind of how that stratification and how the outcomes of young people from deprived backgrounds, for want of a better term, is often really quite poor compared to their peers? Did you be able to kind of access that kind of information? I know, it doesn't make for very good reading. It's quite grim as well.

Amanda: I think, if I understand your question correctly, there are a lot of deficit driven perspectives and actions. So, when a student is in that kind of a segregated space there. The school district and maybe in maybe the community, too, it seemed, at times assumed that they would go from a segregated school setting to a segregated adult setting like a day program or a sheltered workshop. We have sheltered workshops here where folks make very little money over the course of a day to do tasks that are not meaningful and enjoyable necessarily, or that they even have choice over. So, those assumptions were just built in. Even students (with complex support needs) when they graduate high school, they don't necessarily graduate or have to graduate. They stay at high school for several more years to prepare for adulthood but oftentimes the experiences are just the same as when they were high school students.

Misinterpreting legislation and lacking accountability

Joanne: What's the fallout from studies like that? Are there parental advocacy bodies? You know, is there a backlash to that kind of pattern of provision?

Amanda: Backlash from?

Joanne: From, I'm coming from the Irish context, we have disability advocacy bodies that would operate as a voice for parents and young people. We have parental groups as well who would demand a certain standard or campaign for certain supports or facilities to be in place. Does that exist in your context?

Amanda: There are a lot of advocacy groups. I think that at a variety of levels there's a lack of oversight and accountability all the way from the federal government. So that means that local folks are having to fight a fight against other local bodies without the same power or privilege. There's literature here on the misinterpretations of federal law that filters all the way to the state, to the local classroom, to the teacher to student interactions and to the decisions that are being made about IEPs. So, the decisions that are being made there and how our federal laws are interpreted are often not true and miscommunicated to families who may not be certain of their rights or if they are the district is misinterpreting the law, misapplying the law. It's pretty complex.

Susan: And one problem in the states that might be different in Ireland, I know it's different in New Zealand, because I've done some work there as well (Gabel et al., 2009). But, because we're so large and we're so diverse, there isn't really a national consensus about inclusion. And so, we may have a lot of advocacy groups, but some of the advocacy groups are for keeping things the same. They are to, let's say, protect children, to keep children safe, to keep both general education students safe and disabled students. So, there's advocacy on both sides.

We don't have consensus; I don't know if we can reach consensus in a country this large. And so, as Amanda said, everybody's interpreting the law in their own way, and ignoring certain aspects of the law. I can give you a great example. Just today, I was trying to make an argument to my colleagues in our college, that it's inappropriate to get an undergraduate degree in special education, because someone should be a teacher first, able to teach all children and then special education. Because literally, it's a support service to regular education. Special education is something you can add on to your teaching certificate. That's an argument that should have been solved in the 90s in the US. And in 2004, the reauthorization of our federal law should have completely solved the problem. But even in my college, our special education, the way people learn to be special ed teachers is by saying, "Oh, I want to be a special ed teacher, I'm going to get a degree in special ed." Instead of, "I want to be a teacher. I want to learn how to teach. And I'd also like to be able to do this other thing well, too." It would be great if they'd say, "I'd like to be an inclusive teacher." But in Michigan, we have serious constraints over that because of our state regulations and the way we prepare teachers in the state regulations.

Policy influences on teacher education

Joanne: The state regulations informing how you prepare special education teachers?

Susan: The state regulations telling us how we have to prepare special education teachers. And if Amanda disagrees, I really want her to speak to this because she's newer to the state and she has her own ideas. But in our state in particular, the regulations are so strict, down to not just what should be taught to the potential special education teachers, but how many credit hours they should be taught at. It precludes any kind of inclusive teaching between general education and regular teacher preparation. But Amanda, do you see it differently? Maybe I'm being old and you're, you have a more flexible way of looking at things

Amanda: No, I agree. It's incredible to me how much power the state licensure has over what we do at the university. And I think it kind of relates to that language conversation. So, it's how someone else is imagining, how someone else is positioning what disability means and what teachers can do and what students can learn. They're making decisions that impact so many people.

Susan: Other states in our country are able to prepare teachers to be inclusive teachers. So, we have colleagues around the country who developed teacher preparation programs where the teachers leave with both an elementary teacher certification and a special education endorsement.

	That would be ideal. But in Michigan, the regulations make it impossible at this time. If I could figure out how to get around them. I haven't figured that out.
Joanne:	Yeah, it's interesting for me to hear that because as I said before we started recording that there is a bit of a policy disconnect between practice on the ground and the policy in Ireland. But in fairness to the policy community, there's quite a bit of communication between the two. As in, the stakeholders do communicate and even in academia there seems to be communication between academic academia and policy. Is that just not happening?
Susan:	I can only speak to Michigan right now, my other experience was in Chicago, which was a bit different than this. But in Michigan, the policymakers are the politicians. They tell the Department of Education what to do, how to do it. And on the committees that make those decisions or enact those policies, in Michigan there are very few higher education professors. It's mostly teachers, parents, and administrators. Those of us doing research have less influence in in Michigan. What do you think, Amanda?
Amanda:	I would just add that the federal law as written is not strong. It was written that way to be up for interpretation, to grow as the times change, to change as the times change. But we've needed a reauthorization; we haven't had a reauthorization since 2004, and we need one. Folks were worried to do it in the last administration, because of the last federal administration. So hopefully, we'll have a chance soon.
Susan:	So, it's supposed to be reauthorized every five years. So, it's been since 2004, that we haven't had a change. And each reauthorization since 1975, each reauthorization has slowly crept toward the inclusive side of things. So, in 1975, there really wasn't much at all said about it. There really wasn't a right to be in a general education classroom, there was a right to education. And then in the 90s when it was reauthorized, there was a little slow creep towards talking about integration. But then 2004, I thought that was a big reauthorization. And they made it very clear in 2004 that special education is a support service to general education and that students with disabilities have the right to be in the regular classroom. Now, having the right and being able to actually do it are two different things.
Joanne:	We're in a very similar situation here in relation to the UNCRPD (United Nations Convention on the Rights of Persons with Disabilities) in Ireland. We just ratified it in 2018. So, the rights argument has definitely come to the fore more than it ever has before. But at a certain point, students need to be educated and often it's the practicalities that kick in. And by that, can we get into kind of wishful thinking territory? Now I'm going to put to the two of you, what would you like to see? You know, what do you think is the optimum scenario? If we were to kind of park maybe budgetary stuff for the moment? Or what would

you like to see change to ensure a more inclusive education environment for young people with disabilities? And I'm drawing on your earlier study that you mentioned Amanda, students that are different, if you like, from, from the norm for one to better terms.

Amanda: First, I would like for students and families to be positioned as experts. Second, I often feel like a lot of folks just don't know what inclusive education looks like, feels like, and sounds like. Families haven't had experiences and so they're afraid. They don't want their child to be bullied or left out. At the same time, teacher candidates have so few interactions with adults with disabilities as their friends or family members, growing up with peers in scoot that even just imagining what school could be like is difficult. So, I want more opportunities for that to happen. I want us to have more access to be able to dream and recreate education.

Susan: This makes me think about our colleague, Dr. Theo Ressa, who's also in our division. And he has this wonderful, I wish he were here because he says it better than I do. But he talks about the fact that special education should be preparing students to actually fully participate in adult society, in terms of work, that's his emphasis among many other things. Then I think about my two oldest sons, both of whom need around the clock support. One of them is 39 and one of them is 46. Imagine when they went to school, when they were school children, what was happening in their segregated lives, and how little they were prepared for being 39 or 46. And how little they were prepared how little the community was prepared to employ them, to invite them to dinner, to go to a movie with them. I wish that whoever has children in school now, that what has happened to me, and my children won't happen to them. It's quite a struggle. And there are many, many people who are struggling with that. And then we still don't have a support system for what happens to kids after they leave school. As Amanda had said earlier, what if you don't want your child to be in a sheltered workshop? Because you consider that not just segregation, but perhaps cruel, right? Then what do you do with your child? That was one of the dilemmas we ran into. Finding competitive employment is almost impossible for people who need as much support as my kids. So, I just hope that today's parents don't have the same experiences when their children are reaching middle age.

Discussion

While Gabel and Miller came to (special) education via different pathways, there are some commonalities in their identities and experiences as teachers, teacher educators, and disability studies scholars. In this conversation with Joanne, the authors discussed how some aspects of disability discourse, ideology, practice, and policy have changed over time in the US. Often the authors find that misinterpretation of federal legislation and lack of accountability prevent further important, empowering shifts in these realities towards greater inclusivity and equity for youth and adults with disabilities and their families (Turnbull et al., 2007). For example, misinterpretation and misapplication of the least restrictive environment principle of the Individuals with Disabilities Education Improvement Act (IDEA, 2004) is particularly harmful to students with complex support needs and their access to general education classrooms (Gabel et al., 2013; Giangreco, 2019; Kurth et al., 2019). Such misinformation, and the resulting and persistent continuum of services, maintain segregation for students with intellectual and developmental disabilities (Ferguson, 2013). Gabel and Miller also discuss the absence of a nationwide agreement on educational inclusion, particularly for students with complex support needs. While plurality is necessary (Baglieri et al., 2011), this missing national consensus on inclusive education persists in special education research and practice (Taylor et al., 2024; Taylor & Sailor, 2023). Further, these sociopolitical consequences flow into and influence state licensure requirements which can have an enduring impact on university teacher preparation programs (e.g., Young, 2008). As a result, spirals of resistance to change perpetuate the status quo across disability discourse, ideology, practice, and policy.

Conclusion

Despite these ongoing barriers, there is hope and an obligation to find ways to cultivate it in community. The authors center optimism on amplifying student and family experiences, perspectives, and advocacy through critical and participatory frameworks and liberating knowledge disruptions (Naraian & Gabel, 2023; Peters et al., 2009). As such, Gabel and Miller underscore recent scholarship focused on girls of color with complex support needs in middle school and high school and the generative ideas and solutions and creative acts of resistance these youth engage in and share. Centering youth and families, particularly multiply-marginalized families and youth, is vital (Harry & Ocasio-Stoutenberg, 2020; Lalvani & Osieja, 2024; Miller, 2024b). Moreover, such repositioning can disrupt deficit-laden notions about disability and difference and reconstruct schools for more authentically equitable and just educational opportunities and experiences.

References

Baglieri, S., Valle, J. W., Connor, D. J., & Gallagher, D. J. (2011). Disability studies In education: The need for a plurality of perspectives on disability. *Remedial and Special Education*, *32*(4), 267–278. https://doi.org/10.1177/0741932510362200

Ferguson, P. M. (2013). The present king of France is feeble-minded. The logic and history of the continuum of placements for people with intellectual disabilities. In A. S. Kanter & B. A. Ferri (Eds.), *Righting educational wrongs: Disability studies in law and education* (pp. 151–173). Syracuse University Press.

Gabel, S., Cohen, C., Kotel, K., & Pearson, H. (2013). Intellectual disability and space: Critical narratives of exclusion. *Intellectual and Developmental Disabilities*, *51*, 74–80. https://doi.org/10.1352/1934-9556-51.01.074

Gabel, S. L., Curcic, S., Powell, J. J., Khader, K., & Albee, L. (2009). Migration and ethnic group disproportionality in special education: An exploratory study. *Disability & Society*, *24*(5), 625–639. https://doi.org/10.1080/09687590903011063

Giangreco, M. F. (2019). "How can a student with severe disabilities be in a fifth-grade class when he can't do fifth-grade level work?" Misapplying the least restrictive environment. *Research and Practice for Persons with Severe Disabilities*, *45*(1), 23–27. https://journals.sagepub.com/doi/abs/10.1177/1540796919892733

Harry, B., & Ocasio-Stoutenberg, L. (2020). *Meeting families where they are: Building equity through advocacy with diverse schools and communities*. Teachers College Press.

Kurth, J. A., Ruppar, A. L., Toews, S. G., McCabe, K. M., McQueston, J. A., & Johnston, R. (2019). Considerations in placement decisions for students with extensive support needs: An analysis of LRE statements. *Research and Practice for Persons with Severe Disabilities*, *44*(1), 3–19. https://doi.org/10.1177/1540796918825479

Lalvani, P., & Osieja, E. (2024). Battle fatigue: Parents, institutionalized ableism, and the "fight" for inclusive education. *Research and Practice for Persons with Severe Disabilities*. Advanced online publication. https://doi.org/10.1177/15407969241259365

Miller, A. L. (2023). Disabled girls of color excavate exclusionary literacy practices and generate promising sociospatial-textual solutions. *International Journal of Qualitative Studies in Education*, special issue titled "Teaching for inclusion: Complexifying practice with critical disability studies," *36*(2), 247–270. https://doi.org/10.1080/09518398.2020.1828649

Miller, A. L. (2024a). Excavating solutions to sociospatial-textual injustices with girls of color with disabilities in middle school and high school in the United States. In K. Bishop & K. Dimoulias (Eds.), *The Routledge handbook on the influence of built environments on diverse childhoods* (pp. 255–272). Routledge.

Miller, A. L. (2024b). Intersectionality in U.S. educational research: Visibilizing the historically excluded and under-recognized experiences of disabled girls of color. *Educational Review*, *76*(1), 166–180. https://doi.org/10.1080/00131911.2022.2163377

Miller, A. L., & Kurth, J. A. (2022). Photovoice research with disabled girls of color: Exposing how schools (re) produce inequities through school geographies and learning tools. *Disability & Society*, *37*(8), 1362–1390. https://doi.org/10.1080/09687599.2021.1881883

Naraian, S., & Gabel, S. (2023). Teaching for inclusion: Complexifying practice with critical disability studies. *International Journal of Qualitative Studies in Education*, *36*(2), 99–101. https://doi.org/10.1080/09518398.2021.2003902

Peters, S., Gabel, S., & Symeonidou, S. (2009). Resistance, transformation and the politics of hope: Imagining a way forward for the disabled people's movement. *Disability & Society*, *24*(5), 543–556. https://doi.org/10.1080/09687590903010875

Taylor, J. L., Proffitt, W. A., Cornett, J., & Sailor, W. (2024). Unintended consequences of special education and consideration of change. *The Journal of Special Education*, Advanced online publication. https://doi.org/10.1177/00224669241256959

Taylor, J. L., & Sailor, W. (2023). A case for systems change in special education. *Remedial and Special Education*. Advance online publication. https://doi.org/10.1177/07419325231181385

Turnbull, H. R., Stowe, M. J., & Huerta, N. E. (2007). Least restrictive environment. In H. R. Turnbull, M. J. Stowe, & N. E. Huerta (Eds.), *Free appropriate public education* (pp. 205–248). Love Publishing Company.

U.S. Department of Education. (2004). Individuals with disabilities education act. Public Law 108-446. https://www.congress.gov/bill/108th-congress/house-bill/1350/text

Young, K. (2008). "I don't think I'm the right person for that": Theoretical and institutional questions about a combined credential program. *Disability Studies Quarterly*, *28*(4). https://dsq-sds.org/index.php/dsq/article/view/132/132

7
INCLUSION

Musings on process

Srikala Naraian

Introduction

The themes in this chapter arose from a podcast with Dr. Joanne Banks where we discussed a variety of issues related to inclusion. I understand this and the other dialogues that constitute the series to be timely and urgently needed. Even though mainstream special education scholarship has increasingly come to support the inclusion of disabled students in general education classrooms, its conceptual foundations rely on distinguishing ability levels between students to determine where and how they should be educated. In contrast, *inclusive* education begins by inquiring into the ways schooling structures and classroom practice permit (or disallow) students who bring diverse learning profiles (with and without labels of disability) to learn in an equitable manner. *Inclusion* within a disability studies-informed scholarship is a fundamental premise rooted in a democratic orientation to schooling, that acknowledges the diversity of student learning profiles as the norm and requires that educational spaces be designed to reflect this.

Drawing on my own experiences as a researcher and teacher educator, I offer some descriptions that reflect my preoccupation with the element of process within inclusive education (Ainscow, 2007). Specifically, I take up an exploration of inclusion/inclusive education from the perspective of students with the most complex support needs, those who arrive with the labels of "significantly disabled."[1] I subsequently recall my movements as teacher and scholar across Global North-South regions and the ways they have come to inform my approach to inclusion as well as teacher education for inclusion.

Understanding inclusion through significant disability

Inclusive education encompasses all learners deemed "different" by schooling systems. Yet, "difference," need not be located within the individual; rather, inclusive education scholars recognize "difference" as a relational construct that emerges

DOI: 10.4324/9781032705484-8

in the interface of individuals and historically mediated physical and social environments (Dudley-Marling & Burns, 2014; Hart et al., 2004). The difference of *disability* affords a unique opportunity to understand learners. Disability, as an analytic construct, lays bare the *ableist* assumptions of schooling systems that require students to be categorized as "good," "proficient," or "struggling" "at-risk" and so on, as explanations for learning variations. Such variability originates in a variety of experiences that may include displacement, illness, poverty, religious/linguistic minoritization, racial/ethnic trauma, among others. Within pervasively stratified school systems that require such categorization of learners, labels admittedly serve important purposes for students and their families (Ong-Dean, 2009). Still, an approach to inclusion that is derived from such a critical disability lens of "difference," allows us to recognize that at its core, inclusive schooling is about the quest for belonging and membership which has proven foundational to the educational achievement of all learners (Slee, 2019; Lawrence-Brown & Sapon-Shevin, 2014).

My interest in inclusion arose from my early experiences as an educator in an NGO in India with students with complex support needs. My subsequent experiences as a teacher in US public schools continued to develop that experience as it sent me across a range of different education delivery models—the resource room, the self-contained room, the center-based program, and the general education classroom. With each movement, I noticed how the kinds of services that significantly disabled students received were attached to notions of capability and/or conceptions of "severity" of disability, rather than of (re)imaginings of classrooms to accommodate many different kinds of learners. Most of the time, it seemed that students labeled with significant disabilities and their families had to prove to school officials that their child could learn, grow, and develop skills, even if they might look different from their grade-level peers. This also meant that if things did not progress as they hoped it might, schools reverted to the "severe" disability argument or that parents were simply in denial. Not surprisingly, my early research studies were ethnographically oriented investigations into elementary classrooms where students with complex support needs were included (Naraian, 2008, 2010, 2011).

As I observed and learned from the teachers in these classrooms, it seemed clear that significant disability created opportunities in the classroom community for increased student participation and learning. For instance, one student's use of an augmentative communication device informed general norms of participation in the classroom, allowing students with a range of struggles (labeled or unlabeled) to be recognized as equal members by their peers (Naraian et al., 2012). In another classroom, students' engagement with their significantly disabled peers opened up a space for classroom inquiries about disability (Naraian, 2008). The opportunity to interact and build friendships with significantly disabled students allowed students who might find themselves disadvantaged for other reasons (e.g., an English language learner) to participate in the life of the classroom. Learning between significantly disabled students and their peers occurred in unexpected ways, whether it was in musings in journals, in group performances in the music room, or in generous explanations proffered by peers to help the teacher understand a non-speaking student's actions.

Of course, none of this would have occurred without classroom structures that were elastic and where multiple ways of expression were encouraged. When teachers started with a commitment to students with a range of disabilities, their classrooms sparked multiple ways by which those students, including those with complex support needs, could be supported effectively alongside their peers. Such classrooms invited students, families, and support personnel to imagine learning spaces that continually stretched typical assumptions of ability. It contrasted sharply with the curricular context (or the absence thereof) in center-based programs where developing the academic skills of multiple disabled students received less attention than other aspects of their functioning. In these and other classrooms, I have admittedly been struck by the caring stance brought by teachers. Still, in the absence of an expansive vision of disability, care did not translate into innovative practices to enhance student learning and participation.

My inquiries at the high school level to understand inclusion from the perspective of students with the most significant disabilities, disclosed the many cracks within the general education environment that might be implicated in student disengagement (Naraian, 2010). The reliance on lectures not only offers little opportunity for a significantly disabled student to engage with classroom peers and learn academic content. It expects *all* students to learn in the same ways and when they do not, it leaves every student vulnerable to be deemed deficient. In other words, all students are caught within a set of expectations that is predicated on demarcating (in)capability on the basis of narrow measures of learning. This may also be perceived in the numerous "leveled" courses that are offered; students find themselves assigned to sections whose curriculum and pedagogy are premised on the "less capable" student. Additionally, I learnt how the nature of scheduling structures that inhibited the development of peer relations with significantly disabled students equally discouraged the development of relationships between all students.

In some regions, the persistence of these kinds of schooling structures may be attributed to the absence of resources or funding. However, a study conducted with my collaborator (Naraian & Amrhein, 2020) discloses that the effects of (un)availability of resources on inclusive planning are not predictable. In large part, this is because the foundational commitment to inclusion made by administrative leadership varies in depth and conviction. School leaders, who are motivated by a philosophical approach that understands that all learners must be educated together, base their use of available funds on the needs of the schooling community (students, teachers, and families). In some schools, this may take the form of professional development of teachers; in others, it might mean the scheduling of Family Tuesdays when time is allocated weekly for family-teacher meetings during the school day. In still others, it might mean that all classrooms are designated as collaboratively taught, such that a general and a special education teacher are both the lead teachers in each classroom (Naraian et al., 2020). This disrupts the distinctions between "general education classroom" and "special education classroom" permitting instead all classrooms to include students with and without disabilities. In the absence of learning diversity as a foundational value of the school, the arrival of disabled students produces discourses of cost-benefit ratios rather than opportunities to enhance the quality of a community. The significance of funding/resources for promoting inclusion, therefore, cannot be considered apart from the motivations and aspirations of school leaders and school personnel to create particular kinds of school communities.

Inclusion as a traveling reform: Dilemmas of practice

These inquiries established for me the centrality of inclusion as intertwined with the capabilities of the general education structures. It also felt increasingly important to explore the conditions for its enactments. I wanted to come to know inclusion from multiple regional perspectives. Even as I had come to appreciate the importance of a disability rights orientation to disabled students during my years working in an NGO in India, my understanding of inclusion evolved within the debates between general and special education scholars in specifically Western contexts, like the US and UK (Gallagher, 2006). These debates contested the epistemological foundations of special education which were predicated on disability as a deficit within students that then needed to be remediated (Brantlinger, 2005). Inclusion, then, was not just about the placement of disabled students in general education classrooms; it meant recognizing the complicity of both systems—general and special—in creating exclusionary practices (Slee, 2011). Advocating for inclusive practices meant subjecting all elements of the school system, including curriculum, pedagogy, assessments as well as methods of classroom "management" to scrutiny and recognizing the underpinnings of ableism within them.

Even as these efforts towards inclusion came to seem self-evident, I was also acutely conscious of the historically specific contexts in other parts of the world whose educational goals and outcomes were attached to other kinds of socio-economic and political priorities. Increasingly, following the passage of the Salamanca Statement and the United Nations Convention on Rights for Persons with Disabilities (UNCRPD), inclusion was being adopted within various multinational agreements (UNESCO, 1994). I wondered: How was inclusion being taken up in these regions? What relations existed between general and special education systems that fostered or constrained the growth of inclusion? How was inclusion webbed within other national priorities? My early experiences as an educator-activist in India and subsequent role as a researcher/specialist there brought me opportunities to explore these questions. The purpose of these inquiries was not to arrive at the expectation that there could be separate versions of "inclusion" commensurate with the specifics of each regional context. Rather, I wanted to understand how practices in regions that were more likely to be under-resourced and over-whelmed by effects of poverty, low levels of literacy, acute gender inequalities, etc. could stretch the ways that inclusion itself can be imagined for all.

During these experiences, I observed practices that, within strict Northern conceptions of "inclusion," might be described as deficit-based or antithetical to its aims. I heard students, educators, and families repeatedly aspire for "normal" as they moved through the machinery of schooling processes and examinations (Naraian & Natarajan, 2013). I noticed the separation of students based on their abilities/disabilities. I also saw educators working innovatively with impenetrable state-administered examination schedules to ensure that their disabled students might succeed and have an opportunity to attend college. I saw activist educators in disability-centered programs developing linkages with prestigious general education schools to include disabled students. I saw the same educators making difficult decisions about what "kind" of disabled student might most likely be supported to succeed if they were included in that school. Additionally, if those students were significantly disabled, more than likely families would have to be heavily involved in maneuvering the inaccessibility of the physical (and social) environments.

These dilemmas are not unique to Southern regions. My collaborations with researchers in Europe also surfaced similar struggles to stretch mainstream educational structures (Naraian & Amrhein, 2020). Notions of dis/ability were ingrained within the opportunities available to all students. As nation-states in both the Global North and South become signatories to international agreements that promote inclusive education, the means and methods by which inclusive schooling is interpreted and enacted vary. In some regions, educational institutions seek to make policies more disability-inclusive while others may worry about restrictive opportunities for refugee and/or immigrant students. I have learned that each category of learner deemed to show evidence of special educational need—disabled, refugee, out-of-school, out-of-reach, poor, migrant, immigrant—acquires salience within different national contexts through its entanglement in sociopolitical processes unique to that region.

Inevitably, these dilemmas produce forms of schooling practices that differ in terms of the degree of inclusivity (UNESCO, 2018). This unpredictable variability inevitably carries the risk of slippage into exclusionary and/or (in)equitable practices. If the meanings of inclusion are to be locally determined, should one endorse the segregation of some learners (Slee, 2018; Walton, 2018)? Doing so would likely leave untouched the normative foundations of general education systems—what are children being included *into*?—cementing the barriers faced by all children in accessing a meaningful education (Graham & Slee, 2008). At the same time, we also need to consider that any investigation into the variability in meanings of inclusion remains embedded in histories of colonial expansionist policies that have left many nation-states economically and politically disadvantaged within the world order (Tikly, 2004). Such inequalities may be further exacerbated by shifting conditions of living produced via flows of mass migrations, the relentless threat of violence, and the effects of climate change (UNDP, 2019).

These dilemmas remind us that as "inclusion" becomes absorbed into policy rhetoric at different levels, it also runs the risk of becoming an abstract ideal circulating at some distance from everyday struggles and questions. Indeed, global processes such as inclusive schooling agendas come to be seen as "out there" in amorphous space, requiring local enactments "here" within specific geographical locations (Larsen & Beech, 2014). This further promotes understanding of regional responsibilities for inclusion that are assumed to be unidirectional, i.e., we are asked to *implement* pre-given agendas or mandates. Yet, the priorities of local communities must inevitably contend with the economic theories underlying multinational agreements (Tikly, 2019). This likely leads to mutation of central concepts across various planes registering both processes of domination and resistance (Marshall, 2012). Thus, when inquiring into the discrepancies "inclusion" brings forth between global rhetoric and local enactments, we could also wonder: how is locality produced such that global and local forces remain continuously interactive in the moment-to-moment lives of schooling communities (Appadurai, 1996)? A focus on the production of *locality* may permit us to understand variations in inclusive enactments not as a problem, but as an opportunity to expand the scope of "inclusion" itself in order to more capably influence general educational systems.

An attention to global-local processes allows nations considered "behind" to be drawn towards the center of theory-building about inclusion (Acharya, 2018). It refutes notions of passive compliance to external norms to disclose instead the complex workings of agency across multiple planes. Instead, we can consider local agents as actively constructing "foreign" ideas to develop degrees of congruence with local beliefs and practices producing "a two-way dialogue involving the localization of universal ideas and universalizations of local normative and social frameworks" (Acharya, 2018, p. 46). Rather than evaluate regional efforts towards inclusion against norms established in remote places (i.e. the North), investigating processes of "vernacularization" can account for how individuals and institutions participate in the flow of ideas across socio-historical planes (Levitt & Merry, 2009). This can make us mindful of the epistemic dominance inherent in the workings of institutions of higher education in the Global North that has resulted in the erasure of knowledge originating in other regions (Stein, 2017).

Complexifying inclusive teaching practice: Re-centering process

Attuning ourselves to inclusion as a traveling concept within which global and local drivers are always implicated surfaces its inherent complexity as a practice. Within the US (as in many other regions) teachers are caught within discourses of standardization and accountability, leaving educational procedures and practices at risk for ableist exclusions (Labaree, 2014). Serving as a teacher educator for the last seventeen years, I see a linkage between the absence of locality within global discourses of inclusion and the expectations for inclusive practice placed on teachers. It is centered on the importance of the element of *process*. Even as *process* has been clearly delineated in descriptions of inclusive education (Ainscow, 2007), it has been inadequately folded into theories and imaginings of how inclusion may be enacted by teachers, schools, and policy-makers. In other words, inclusion as a set of desired practices remains the standard against which schools and educators are to be assessed. This creates categories as "heroic" or "compliant" "successful" "unsuccessful" within which teachers, schools, or even regions must be located, perpetuating the same deficit orientation that inclusion seeks to evade.

A deliberate focus on process directs us away from locating problems of practice within teachers or schools and invites us to think about the ways other discourses, events, and practices affect the ways in which inclusion may be enacted. To clarify, the enactment of inclusion begins with an unapologetic commitment to making the educational environment hospitable to all learners, regardless of the various labels attached to them. Still, promoting inclusive practice requires a recognition of how such commitments may be at risk of being continually eroded by contextually specific conditions including accountability mandates for teachers and students, federal policies of funding, the threat of privatization, restrictive policies of immigration, migrant labor practices, and state-sponsored surveillance of curriculum, to name a few. The conditions under which teachers' inclusive practice must be enacted therefore are complex and call for complex theorizing of inclusion itself. Said differently, the concept of inclusion is inseparable from the process by which it is enacted.

What, then, does teaching for inclusion mean? How can a commitment to inclusive enactments merge with a commitment to teacher growth and learning? Teachers' agency for realizing inclusion arises from ecologies of practice that include situational factors as well as their own evolution over time (Priestly et al., 2016). Their embeddedness within various professional communities may or may not adequately sustain the commitments derived from their teacher education programs. Yet, professional development for inclusion may also not be accomplished through intermittent one-shot approaches, requiring instead sustained guided support over time. Such an approach centers teachers' experiences, privileging their stories of coming to know (Cochran-Smith & Lytle, 2009). This is a shift from the traditional emphasis within the field of inclusive education that has typically made the experiences of disabled students and their families central to coming to know inclusion. To investigate enactments of inclusion arguably requires that we learn to straddle these priorities, without, of course, neglecting the attachments to equity that animate our research and teaching.

Attaching value to teachers' stories discloses the contradictory threads that pervade the work of inclusion. As they work with families who bring multiple orientations to school and learning, teachers must move between multiple ideological positions whether in their pedagogy (e.g. constructivist/behaviorist) or in the recommendations they make about student placement (e.g. inclusive/self-contained).

Their decision-making comes from a range of processes that implicate both a concern for student learning as well as the grammar of schooling that upholds particular conceptions of time and place (Tyack & Cuban, 1997). Inclusion, in these instances, is neither readily recognizable nor is it easily categorizable. Without an acknowledgement of the interconnected processes on different planes that produce enactments of inclusion, our imaginings of this elusive and ephemeral concept are at risk of remaining out-of-sync with rapidly shifting political, social, and material environments in which teachers teach and students learn.

Finally, a recognition of the process directs us to acknowledge that teaching for inclusion itself is subsumed within the larger field of teacher education. However, a sustained and in-depth conversation between the fields of teacher education and disability studies-informed inclusive education continues to remain tentative at best, and completely missing at worst (Cosier & Pearson, 2016). This remains an area of some importance, as we continue to inquire into the complexities of teaching inclusively. Conceptions of ability undergird standards of dispositions, skills, and knowledge on which professional assessments of teachers' competence are based. The narratives of teachers with disabilities challenge those assumptions and call for us to embed ourselves more deeply within teacher education processes (Wood, 2022). This allows questions of (in)competence, (in)ability, disability, and inclusion/exclusion to infiltrate broader discourses of teacher education blunting a reliance on special education for addressing the same.

Note

1 For convenience, I use the term "significantly disabled" and "students with complex support needs" interchangeably. However, I also follow McRuer (2006) who uses a related term–"severely disabled"– not so much to signify bodies that are most incapacitated, but rather as those that are most suitably positioned to disclose the "inadequacies of compulsory ablebodiedness" (p. 31). The "significant" in "significant disability" therefore is well-suited to my purpose to understand inclusion from the perspectives of those most marginalized in schools.

References

Acharya, A. (2018). *Constructing global order: Agency and change in world politics* Cambridge University Press.

Ainscow, M. (2007). Taking an inclusive turn. *Journal of Research in Special Educational Needs*, 7(1), 3–7.

Appadurai, A. (1996). *Modernity at large: Cultural dimensions of globalization*. University of Minnesota Press.

Brantlinger, E. (2005). *Who benefits from special education?* Lawrence Erlbaum.

Cochran-Smith, M., & Lytle, S. L. (2009). *Inquiry as stance: Practitioner research for the next generation*. Teachers College Press.

Cosier, M., & Pearson, H. (2016). Can we talk? The underdeveloped dialogue between teacher education and disability studies. *SAGE Open*, 6(1). https://doi.org/10.1177/2158244015626766

Dudley-Marling, C., & Burns, M. B. (2014). Two perspectives on inclusion in the United States. *Global Education Review*, *1*(1), 14–31.

Gallagher, D. J. (2006). The natural history undone: Disability studies' contributions to contemporary debates in education. In S. Danforth & S. L. Gabel (Eds.), *Vital questions facing disability studies in education* (vol. 2, pp. 63–75). Peter Lang.

Graham, L., & Slee, R. (2008). An illusory interiority: Interrogating the discourse/s of inclusion. *Educational Philosophy and Theory*, *40*(2), 277–293.

Hart, S., Dixon, A., Drummond, M. J., & McIntyre, D. (2004). *Learning without limits*. Open University Press.

Labaree, D. F. (2014). Let's measure what no one teaches: PISA, NCLB and the shrinking aims of education. *Teachers College Record*, *116*, 1–14.

Larsen, M. A., & Beech, J. (2014). Spatial theorizing in comparative and international education research. *Comparative Education Review*, *58*(2), 191–214.

Lawrence-Brown, D., & Sapon-Shevin, M. (2014). *Condition critical: Key principles for equitable and inclusive education*. Teachers College Press.

Levitt, P., & Merry, S. (2009). Vernacularization on the ground: Local uses of global women's rights in Peru, China, India and the United States. *Global Networks*, *9*(4), 441–461.

Marshall, N. (2012). Digging deeper: The challenge of problematizing 'inclusive' development and 'disability mainstreaming. In A. Bletass & C. Beasley (Eds.), *Engaging with Carol Bacchi: Strategic interventions and exchanges* (pp. 53–70). University of Adelaide Press.

McRuer, R. (2006). *Crip theory: Cultural signs of queerness and disability*. NYU Press.

Naraian, S. (2008). "I didn't think I was going to like working with him, but now I really do!" Examining peer narratives of significant disability. *Intellectual and Developmental Disabilities*, *46*(2), 106–119.

Naraian, S. (2010). Disentangling the social threads in a communicative environment: A cacophonous tale of alternative and augmentative communication (AAC). *European Journal of Special Needs Education*, *25*(3), 253–267.

Naraian, S. (2011). Seeking transparency: The production of an inclusive classroom community. *International Journal of Inclusive Education*, *15*(9), 955–973.

Naraian, S., & Amrhein, B. (2020). Learning to read 'inclusion' divergently: Enacting a transnational approach to inclusive education. *International Journal of Inclusive Education*, *26*(14), 1327–1346. https://doi.org/10.1080/13603116.2020.1807624

Naraian, S., Chacko, M., Feldman, C., & Schwitzman-Gerst, T. (2020). Emergent concepts of inclusion in the context of committed school leadership. *Education and Urban Society*, *52*(8), 1238–1263.

Naraian, S., Ferguson, D. L. & Thomas, N. (2012). Transforming for inclusive practice: Professional development to support the inclusion of students labeled as emotionally disturbed. *International Journal of Inclusive Education*, *16*(7–8), 721–740.

Naraian, S., & Natarajan, P. (2013). Negotiating normalcy with peers in contexts of inclusion: Perceptions of youth with disabilities in India. *International Journal of Disability, Development and Education*, *60*(2), 146–166. https://doi.org/10.1080/1034912X.2013.786565

Ong-Dean, C. (2009). *Distinguishing disability: Parents, privilege and special education*. University of Chicago Press.

Priestly, M., Biesta, G., & Robinson, S. (2016). *Teacher agency: An ecological approach*. Bloomsbury.

Slee, R. (2011). *The irregular school: Exclusion, schooling, and inclusive education*. Routledge.

Slee, R. (2018). *Inclusive Education Isn't Dead, it Just Smells Funny*. Routledge

Slee, R. (2019). Belonging in an age of exclusion. *International Journal of Inclusive Education*, *23*(9), 909–922.

Stein, S. (2017). The persistent challenges of addressing epistemic dominance in higher education: Considering the case of curriculum internationalization. *Comparative Education Review*, *61*(S1), 25–50.

Tikly, L. (2004). Education and the new imperialism. *Comparative Education, 4*(2), 173–198.
Tikly, L. (2019). Education for sustainable development in Africa: *A critique of regional agendas. Asia Pacific Education Review, 20*(2), 223–237. https://doi.org/10.1007/s12564-019-09600-5
Tyack, D. B., & Cuban, L. (1997). *Tinkering towards Utopia: A century of educational reform*. Harvard University Press.
UNDP (2019). *Beyond income, beyond averages, beyond today: Inequalities in human development in the 21st century*. Human Development Report 2019. UNDP, New York, NY.
UNESCO (1994). *The Salamanca statement and framework for action on special needs education*. UNESCO.
UNESCO (2018) *Global Education Meeting 2018: Education in an interconnected world; ensuring inclusive and equitable development* https://unesdoc.unesco.org/notice?id=p::u smarcdef_0000366339
Walton, E. (2018). Decolonising (through) inclusive education? *Educational Research for Social Change, 7*, 31–45.
Wood, R. (2022). *Learning from autistic teachers: How to be a neuro-diversity inclusive school*. Jessica Kingsley.

8
LEARNING FROM OTHERS

Comparing institutionalizations of special and inclusive education

Justin J.W. Powell

Introduction

Inclusive education has become an increasingly discussed dimension of education globally over recent decades. However, while comparative studies in education research, policy, and practice have gained importance, such insights remain underutilized in the fields of inclusive and special education. This is surprising, given that learning from others through comparative data and analyses is essential to address important theoretical, methodological, and practical questions (Powell, 2020).

Increasingly, inclusive education is recognized as a human right and a global norm—and has become a contentious policy field. The concept of "inclusion" is understood differently across contexts, which impacts policy discourse and implementation. The contrasts reflect the intertwined institutionalizations of special and inclusive education. Paradoxically, in many places, segregated or separate educational settings continue to exist or have even expanded, even where the explicit goal has been to bolster inclusion (Biermann, 2022; Richardson & Powell, 2011). On multiple levels, we face ongoing challenges but also have opportunities for inspiration and improvement by leveraging the findings of comparative studies of institutional and organizational persistence and change in special and inclusive education (Köpfer et al., 2021).

Inclusive education has emerged as a key theme in global education over the past decades, not least due to educational expansion at all levels, the global disability movement, and human rights mandates—as well as increased action and advocacy by international organizations and supranational governance. This field, building upon the approaches and insights of many disciplines and methods, addresses contentious issues of educational equity; dis/ability, difference, and difference; learning opportunities; and the organization of schooling.

DOI: 10.4324/9781032705484-9

Building upon the interview with Joanne Banks (2022) in her *The Inclusion Dialogue* podcast series (see also Banks, 2023), this chapter summarizes findings from comparative institutional analyses of education systems relating to special and inclusive education.[1] The United States, the country of my birth and primary socialization, was earlier than many in forcefully embracing rights-based "inclusive" education, originally called "mainstreaming". Growing up in the American South in the 1970s, I attended schools that had only recently been desegregated, racially. Children with disabilities would be the next group to be integrated into public schools, which required similar struggle and social change—still necessary and ongoing. Under protection from the *Education of All Handicapped Children Act* of 1975 (now known as the *Individuals with Disabilities Education Act*, IDEA), my twin brother Martin was among the first "mainstreamed" children in Charlottesville, Virginia, yet only after the local school district was forced to devise necessary accommodations; he began elementary school several years later. He tells his own story in his book *Living at the Heart of the UVA Community* (Powell, 2018). Growing up acutely aware of stigmatization and institutionalized discrimination shaped our understanding of social exclusion and inclusion and of institutional persistence and change in education. Germany, the country in which my academic career was shaped, provides a notable contrast. A pioneer in special education (as in many other aspects of schooling) over a century ago, Germany reduced the exclusion of children with various impairments and disabilities, as it expanded compulsory schooling. Today, despite its ratification of the UN Convention on the Rights of People with Disabilities (UN CRPD) in 2008, many of Germany's states (*Länder*) continue to teach most pupils "with special educational needs" (SEN) in segregated special schools. Others have embraced inclusive education and gradually institutionalized these programmes over the past decades (Powell et al., 2016). In both federal countries, state-level differences are considerable, showing that even within a country, diverse pathways towards the ideal of inclusion are typical—and these systems continuously change incrementally, not always resulting in more inclusion. A historical-comparative account was elaborated in *Barriers to Inclusion: Special Education in the United States and Germany* (Powell, 2011/2016). Here, I summarize results of numerous comparative research projects on special and inclusive education in Europe.

Analysing inclusive education as global norm from comparative and life course perspectives

Compulsory schooling and paid work are considered "normal" life stages in most societies but remain uncertain for many disabled people. Despite the increasing importance of education, some students—especially those who have participated in special education—still face discrimination, leave school without qualifications, and encounter difficulties transitioning to work, reducing their life chances and well-being. Paradoxically, as educational expectations and aspirations rise worldwide (Baker, 2014), more students participate in special education, which often exacerbates disadvantage as it often hinders successful transitions from school-to-work (Powell, 2006). Life course approaches emphasize the importance of analysing the cumulative dis/advantages (Powell, 2011/2016).

Special education, expanded especially during the late twentieth century, initially aimed to support children with recognized impairments but has since expanded to include those with a variety of SEN, like learning disabilities, that reflect changing expectations for school success. As many of these students with SEN, often from disadvantaged backgrounds, do not receive schooling "without discrimination and on the basis of equal opportunity" (UN CRPD, Article 24), this conflicts with the human right to inclusive education. Even as all European countries have ratified the UN CRPD, many struggle to achieve full inclusion, with Nordic and Southern European countries having advanced considerably, showing the possibilities in very different cultural contexts (and with different ideals, resources, and governance) (Powell et al., 2019).

Inclusive education, grounded in human rights (Heyer, 2021), has become a global norm, emphasizing the right to education for all in diverse societies across the continents. Yet, the task of addressing student diversity in classrooms and enhancing accessibility remains a challenge for teachers everywhere. Significant differences in the extent and quality of inclusive education across Europe reflect varied institutional structures and practices (European Parliament 2017). Since the worldwide ratification of the UN CRPD, defining inclusive education as a lifelong right, schools have faced pressure to develop inclusive cultures, structures, and practices (Ainscow, 2023). Furthermore, the 2030 Agenda for Sustainable Development highlights quality education as a key goal (SDG 4) (United Nations 2015), with progress monitored by UNESCO (2020). Comparative research is crucial to track progress towards these goals (Powell, 2020).

Understanding these issues requires continuous dialogue and historical comparative studies of different schools, systems, and cultures (Artiles et al., 2011; Richardson & Powell, 2011). Responses to the educational and social disadvantages faced by students with SEN or those who "become disabled" during schooling depend on how education and welfare systems are structured and their resources. While outright exclusion has been reduced through special education, these programs often remain separate from general education and lead to stigmatization. In many contexts, children from low-income backgrounds, boys, ethnic minorities, and children from migrant families are (considerably) overrepresented in such programs (Tomlinson, 2017).

Diverse approaches in a multidisciplinary field

Within the multidisciplinary field of educational research, sociological approaches to disability, and special and inclusive education emphasize themes like exclusion/inclusion, segregation/integration, in/equalities, institutionalization, stigma, learning opportunities, risk, as well as accessibility, achievement, and attainment. Studies of special and inclusive education and their interrelation (see Florian, 2019) enhance our understanding of how disability and SEN are constructed (categories and classification systems), often rooted in deficit-oriented medical or clinical frameworks, and how these relate to educational opportunities and outcomes. They manifest the challenging, often unintended, consequences of participating in special education programs. Research linking educational attainment to social stratification and employing a life course perspective highlights how early inequities shape life chances; however, limited representative and longitudinal data on this diverse minority group hinder a full understanding of the negative effects of stigmatization and segregation (see Blanck, 2020; Pfahl, 2011; Powell, 2006). This challenge persists due to the complexity of education systems, the path-dependent nature of special education structures, and complex multi-level governance, especially in federal countries (Powell, 2011; Powell et al., 2016).

Education is central to nation-states' governance and their economies, as it shapes not only political values but also the capabilities of future workers, especially given rapid technological advances. Compulsory schooling laws were initially introduced to socialize citizens and prepare them for the workforce (Heidenheimer, 1997). Education, largely state-funded, signals a universal policy investing in citizens' capabilities and the future workforce. By providing free and compulsory public education, democratic nations affirm the close relationship between education and citizenship (Marshall, 1950/1992). As nation-states industrialized and citizenship rights expanded, mass schooling arose alongside the cultural ideologies of the nation-state (Boli et al., 1985). Globally, education increasingly determines individual identities and life chances, as we grow up in "schooled societies" (Baker, 2014). Yet, in many contexts, children and young adults have been excluded from this universal policy, resulting in significant disadvantages and reduced well-being (Richardson & Powell, 2011). Paradoxically, as participation, achievement, and attainment rates have risen, these vulnerable groups are increasingly stigmatized and disadvantaged (Solga, 2002).

At the macro and meso-levels, the construction of disability categories and the organization of school settings play a critical role in determining who receives targeted support and services. These institutions and organizations shape the experiences of young people classified as disabled at the micro level. Organizations operate within distinct "institutional logics" (Thornton et al., 2012), and individuals must adapt to these differing values, practices, and expectations. These logics become particularly relevant as individuals transition from school to work, requiring different forms of performance (Tschanz & Powell, 2020). The types and qualities of support provided often vary significantly. In education, there is a tension between providing necessary additional support or specialized services while avoiding the risk of stigmatization (thus, some systems attempt to reduce or forego classification). Receiving such services may carry positive or, more likely, negative connotations, especially when an official classification is required, a dilemma referred to as the "resource-labelling dilemma" (Füssel & Kretschmann, 1993). Welfare state institutions complicate this further by structuring ambiguous and inconsistent disability classification systems, where access to resources is tied to official medical, legal, or pedagogical definitions. This creates a "distributive dilemma" (Stone, 1984) in which policymakers and street-level bureaucrats and other gatekeepers must balance the need-based, targeted distribution of additional supports and conferring categorical membership that can exclude or marginalize individuals. What insights can current research on inclusive education provide about the origins of these dilemmas and paradoxes?

Education systems' institutional design & factors affecting transitions

The institutional design of education systems significantly impacts the potential for inclusive education, learning, and well-being for all students. The institutionalization of these systems dictates the types of learning settings available, each differing in aspiration level and class composition. Key features shaping the school landscape include educational opportunities across levels, from early childhood education through to vocational and higher education and lifelong learning as well as the degree of stratification within and between educational stages, such as the number of parallel school tracks, especially at the secondary level. Education systems also differ considerably in their "permeability"—or how easily students can move between school types or levels, for example, from more vocationally to more academically oriented programs (Bernhard & Graf, 2022).

Although special education programs have integrated students with recognized impairments or SEN into the broader education system, these students often face stigmatization and segregation, which contributes to their disablement (Powell, 2011/2016). The factors influencing transitions from school to work are complex. Learning opportunities within schools, VET programs, and workplaces support development, while state programs and social networks provide crucial information and assistance. However, gatekeepers' recruitment practices can introduce bias, contributing to "institutional discrimination" (Gomolla & Radtke, 2002). Although individual motivation, competencies, and decision-making play key roles (Ludwig-Mayerhofer et al., 2019), large and persistent differences across education systems highlight the impact of categorical definitions of SEN and the limited opportunities available to students. These factors lead to widely varying rates of experiencing disablement, even for students within the same SEN category.

Transitions from school to work are particularly challenging, as highlighted by comparisons, such as between the U.S. and Switzerland (Tschanz & Powell, 2020). Success in navigating these transitions is crucial for life chances, with skill formation programs, especially VET, playing a pivotal role in supporting labour market integration. These aim to build bridges between education and employment, can promote successful transitions and thus inclusion; however, they must attempt to compensate for previous disablement and cumulative disadvantages in learning opportunities.

Comparative perspectives on inclusive education: Global norms and local paradoxes

Despite the increasing importance of comparative analysis in educational research, policymaking, and practice, these approaches have not yet received the attention they deserve in the fields of inclusive and special education. Comparative and international perspectives are essential for addressing key theoretical, methodological, and practical issues, yet they remain underutilized. Both international organizations and (supra)national governments have increasingly focused on recognizing diversity and promoting Education for All (EfA). This agenda, which gained visibility with the Salamanca Declaration (UNESCO, 1994), has since spread worldwide, reinforced by the Sustainable Development Goals (SDGs) (UNESCO, 2022). Almost all countries have ratified the UN Convention on the Rights of Persons with Disabilities (UN CRPD) (United Nations, 2006), which was developed and demanded by disability rights activists and advocates globally and mandates the establishment of inclusive education systems across all ages and educational levels, from early childhood to lifelong learning.

This international framework is significant not only in shaping definitions, curricular content, and pedagogy but also in promoting the global norm of inclusive education as a human right. However, the concept of inclusion and what constitutes educational equity remain subjects of debate, with differing interpretations and implications across national and local contexts. This has led to a paradox where segregated or separate settings have been maintained—or even expanded—under the banner of inclusion (see, e.g. Biermann, 2022, on Germany and Nigeria). Such contradictions raise questions about the efficiency, equity, and true inclusiveness of these systems.

Mapping the geography of special and inclusive education across Europe

Across Europe, there are significant differences in how students with SEN are classified and disparities in the groups served, revealing stark contrasts in education systems, the values underpinning them, and their institutionalization. European data that highlight these differences come from the European Agency for Special Needs and Inclusive Education (EASNIE, https://www.european-agency.org/activities/data), which provides comparative data across 31 European countries (see Ramberg & Watkins, 2020). Collected from member countries, these indicators show both general trends and contrasting patterns of educational differentiation and settings provided for students with SEN. This allows comparisons on the rates and types of SEN classification as well as the proportion of students educated in the continuum of settings, from segregated to fully inclusive. Recent data (2020/2021) shows that SEN classification rates range from less than 1% to nearly 17% of the student population, with a European average just over 4%. Extraordinary, this variation reflects the institutionalization of (special and inclusive) education, especially the diverse definitions and categories of SEN, and the unequal distribution of educational resources and opportunities in various settings (EASNIE, 2024; Richardson & Powell, 2011).

Case studies from countries in all parts of Europe—Germany, Iceland, Lithuania, Luxembourg, Spain, and Sweden—showcase both opportunities and challenges of creating inclusive education systems (TdiverS Project, see Powell et al., 2019). While some schools successfully implement inclusive practices, these are rarely scaled up to the national level, especially when the logic of the system is not inclusive. Even within the Nordic region, with among the most inclusive systems in Europe, Sweden's classification rate is as low as 0.5%, while Iceland's reaches over 16%, highlighting how differently countries—even in the same region—define SEN and distribute resources. Such disparities are reinforced by the ongoing reliance on clinical definitions of disability, which in turn influence the services and support provided to students with SEN, but party politics and education and social policymaking also impact the fate and future of inclusive education (Taneja-Johansson & Powell, 2024).

Although global norms, such as those embedded in the UN CRPD, promote inclusive education, many countries still maintain segregated schools or separate classrooms. Italy maintains one of the lowest segregation rates, with nearly all students, including those with SEN, placed in inclusive mainstream settings. Countries like Iceland and Spain also report low segregation rates, indicating their strong commitment to inclusive education settings and practices. In contrast, Germany and Belgium show higher rates of segregation, with up to 7% of students with SEN educated in separate or specialized settings. This aligns with historical and systemic tendencies within their education systems that favour more forms of support not provided in general education. Contemporary *European Agency Statistics on Inclusive Education (EASIE)* underscore that while inclusive education is a widely shared goal, countries continue to adopt diverse approaches in practice, which influences the overall rate of segregated placements. These findings highlight ongoing challenges in harmonizing inclusive education efforts across Europe to provide equitable learning opportunities for all students, including those with SEN. These disparities reflect deeper structural and cultural differences across countries. Even among nations committed to inclusive education, such as those in the Nordic region, there is a lack of consistency in how inclusive practices are defined and implemented (e.g. Biermann & Powell, 2014). Recent political shifts, such as in Sweden, have put further pressure on inclusive education, with policy changes leading to increased diagnosis, higher classification rates, and more separate provision, influenced by more general policies oriented towards markets and decentralization (Taneja-Johansson & Powell, 2024).

This variation underscores the importance of addressing both the structural barriers to inclusion and the challenges posed by segregated settings, which can limit educational attainment and (re)produce social disadvantage. Ultimately, this highlights the need for evidence-based policy reforms to make education systems more inclusive. Comparative studies, like the EU Project Teaching Diverse Learners in School Subjects (TdiverS), help identify "inspiring practices" (Powell et al., 2019) and areas for improvement. Yet the pathways towards truly inclusive education remain complex, with many countries facing persistent challenges in balancing the provision of resources and support with the risks of stigmatization and separation.

International and intranational comparisons emphasize that education systems develop in "path-dependent" ways, with various barriers and facilitators, such as acknowledging and realizing the human right to inclusive education (Powell et al., 2016). Comparative studies of the development of inclusive education frequently refer to the policy recommendations of international organizations and of other countries, particularly those like Canada, Norway, and Italy that since the 1990s have further developed their systems' inclusiveness (see, e.g. contributions in Köpfer et al., 2021). To understand the barriers to inclusion and how to overcome them, we must analyse the institutionalization of segregated and separate school settings as well as the drivers behind the convergence to the "continuum" of educational settings (see Powell, 2011/2016). The myriad negative consequences of lessened learning opportunities and stigmatization for individuals and societies alike demand both more evidence-based policymaking and more critical reflection because the transformation required to implement fully inclusive systems requires sustained activism and advocacy.

Change in education is often gradual and increment. Despite considerable differences in education systems across Europe, inclusive educational practices are everywhere to be found at the school level. Building upon the TdiverS project in comparative education research, including school site visits (Powell et al., 2019), we found inspiring "inclusive practices" in Germany, Iceland, Lithuania, Luxembourg, Spain, and Sweden, despite their contrasting overall levels of inclusive education and education systems more generally. While Europe has diverse cultures and languages, the desire for cooperation across boundaries, be it cultural, linguistic, disciplinary, or professional, was evident—as was the need to collaborate to successfully understand inclusive practices and facilitate them in such diverse contexts. The project highlighted the need to consider multiple levels of education systems—local, regional, and national—since aggregated national data often does not reflect lower-level realities. Some schools, even in highly segregated systems, are actively moving towards inclusion, defying the broader system's tendency to maintain special education as separate. Another key barrier is the persistence of segregated educational settings. Despite global normative pressures, such as the UN CRPD, convergence towards fully inclusive education remains limited. National reforms must address the deeply institutionalized nature of special education if meaningful progress is to be made towards more inclusive systems across Europe.

Inclusive education reforms: From policy initiatives to sustainability in schools?

In charting the development of inclusive education reforms especially, scientific attention to the gap between policy rhetoric that often subscribes to human rights and international norms in education (as codified in the UN CRPD's Article 24, or the Sustainable Development Goals, i.e. SDG 4 Quality Education) and system and school realities is crucial. The normative dimension of human rights charters has succeeded in broad-based awareness-raising about inclusive education but has also called forth countervailing forces and even backlash (Powell et al., 2016). Yet even in the most successfully inclusive contexts, school leaders and teachers require support, resources, and networking opportunities across borders as they become change agents and maintain support for the gradual and continual process of fostering inclusion. This valorizes the schools' provision and practices in the face of contrasting system logics: inclusive schooling is not compatible with segregated structures and settings, yet these remain ubiquitous in many countries. Thus, inherently, inclusive education must be realized as an ongoing (political) process and as a goal, rather than a once attained and stable status. The challenges for inclusion are historically and regionally shifting, as they relate to contexts and therefore differ according to (levels within) education systems. As a process, it is inherently challenging, with political implications. If comparative studies emphasize that many of these questions asked across Europe are similar, no school or country is alone in answering them.

Where such reforms have progressed, they should not be taken for granted, as these reform processes and the inclusive values undergirding them are always at risk of being stopped or rescinded. Thus, researchers, policymakers, and practitioners must attend to the sustainability of the implementation of reforms aiming to make schooling more inclusive. Modelling inclusion in schools was found important, namely for all involved to "live" inclusion, including such features as neighbourhood outreach programs, students' and parents' active participation in school development, school charters signed by all members of the school, ethical leadership, and team-teaching to provide adult role models for collaboration and inclusive practices within the school (Powell et al., 2019). Indeed, a key method for bolstering the sustainability of inclusive schooling is to rely on the dialogic principle, ensuring communication among all stakeholders and all those participating in the life of the school and the education of the next generation. Next, I discuss the implementation of inclusive education and additional lessons learned from comparative perspectives.

Implementing inclusive education across Europe

Comparative research highlights the diversity of learners everywhere as well as cross-national and within-country differences and disparities in learning opportunities, all of which relate to the varying stages of implementation of inclusive education reforms. From a systemic perspective, inclusive education can be viewed as an overarching change initiative aimed at transforming educational structures, cultures, and practices (Ainscow, 2023). In more inclusive systems, advancing inclusion involves eliminating the separation of students into ability-based groups and providing individual support within general classrooms. In less inclusive contexts, developments such as ambulatory services provide short-term solutions by minimizing the need for segregation, delivering support services to individual students. However, special schools persist across all European countries (see Ramberg & Watkins, 2020), with some, like Germany, serving the majority of students with SEN in these settings, while others, such as Iceland, Lithuania, Luxembourg, Spain, and Sweden, serve only a (very) small group. Nonetheless, classification rates, as discussed above, vary considerably across these nations.

The spatial aspect of schooling is vital, as schools should function as supportive environments that offer diverse learning opportunities and promote well-being and embeddedness in communities. Implementing inclusive principles necessitates changes to curricula and school culture, fostering an environment open to and fostering community. Teachers in countries with comprehensive schooling systems that accommodate all pupils typically have more experience teaching heterogeneous groups than those in stratified systems with multiple secondary school types. Regarding learning processes, assessments for learning and diagnostics have come to play critical roles as either barriers or facilitators of inclusion. Competence-focused assessments often adopt a deficit-oriented approach that leads to labelling, in turn making stigmatization more likely. Emphasizing the importance of individualized education plans, some schools have successfully reduced their reliance on competence measures and developed alternative assessments, such as portfolio work, with this approach encouraging peer-to-peer interaction and collaborative learning among all students (Noesen, in press). However, challenges arise, especially during transitions, due to prevailing systemic norms, underscoring the need for inclusive education to be pursued as a comprehensive, system-wide reform. Furthermore, traditional subject teaching may limit inclusion compared to multidisciplinary, project-based approaches that foster inclusivity.

Discussion: Implications for inclusive education research and policymaking

Reviewing the above presented harmonized data of key indicators and selected cross-national comparative studies, we find that descriptive aggregate statistics mask paradoxes, such as the professional engagement in and development of inclusive education and co-teaching without declining rates of special schooling overall (Germany). Even in a system of inclusive, student-centred, collaboration-oriented schools, equalizing opportunities and improving student well-being remains a key goal for school development (Iceland). When teachers support learners as collaborative partners, especially in well-resourced, more personalized, and accessible classrooms, schooling improves (Lithuania). Inclusion from an intersectional perspective and dialogic teaching in culturally diverse, multilingual schools is facilitated by alternative assessments, portfolio work, and student-centred pedagogy (Luxembourg). The values of inclusion and ethical leadership to foster collaboration among all stakeholders is crucial for inclusive education to develop over the long run (Spain). Students are ready to respect diversity, promote tolerance, and support solidarity, which fosters inclusive education that in turn facilitates equality *and* achievement (Sweden). The significance of these findings derived from research and practice has been published as material for teacher education in English and the half-dozen languages represented by the TdiverS Project partner countries, including a collection of multilingual videography and multidisciplinary resources (see www.tdivers.eu).

Cross-national collaborative projects promote in-depth comparison, cooperation, and understanding among representatives of countries with contrasting education systems and very different institutionalization pathways towards inclusive schooling. Such exchange proves crucial in ongoing inclusive education research and reform. In these six countries, professionals in schools, families, and students emphasized the need to work together and exchange perspectives, with even the already most inclusive schools and communities regarding inclusion more as a continuous process of renewal than as an attained status. Resources from multiple sources and networking opportunities across organizational and institutional borders bolster progress in realizing more inclusive schooling. This is especially important in those contexts in which system logics remains focused on placement in special settings, which is incompatible with inclusive schooling (for example, the logic in the United States is separation, in Germany segregation, see Powell, 2011/2016). This also emphasizes the politics surrounding inclusive education, especially as the goals and challenges shift in an era of "education for all" and inclusive education as a human right (UNESCO, 2020), but with contemporary politics often questioning the democratic tenets of inclusive education. Comparisons provide learning opportunities to recognize similarities in the challenges faced that are ubiquitous across all levels, while differently successful reforms and "inspiring practices" from elsewhere serve as models and support for innovation.

If inclusive reforms have progressed across Europe, at different paces and to different extents, they should not be taken for granted, but rather valorized and protected. Practitioners, administrators, researchers, and policymakers are responsible for ensuring the sustainability of implemented reforms that aim to make schooling more inclusive and meet the SDGs. Such change is in accord with the global norm of inclusive education as a human right and recognizes the benefits of diversity and equity in education.

Note

1 Inclusion Dialogue with Joanne Banks, March 3, 2022. https://podcasts.apple.com/us/podcast/inclusion-dialogue/id1541011089

References

Ainscow, M. (2023). Making sense of inclusion and equity in education: A personal journey. In J. Banks (Ed.), *The inclusion dialogue: Debating issues, challenges and tensions with global experts* (pp. 6–22). Routledge.
Artiles, A. J., Kozleski, E., & Waitoller, F. R. (Eds.) (2011). *Inclusive education. Examining equity on five continents*. Harvard Education Press.
Baker, D. P. (2014). *The schooled society*. Stanford University Press.
Banks, J. (2022). The Inclusion Dialogue: Interview with Justin Powell. March 3, 2022. https://podcasts.apple.com/us/podcast/inclusion-dialogue/id1541011089
Banks, J. (2023). *The inclusion dialogue: Debating issues, challenges and tensions with global experts*. Routledge.
Bernhard, N., & Graf, L. (2022). Enhancing permeability through cooperation. In G. Bonoli & P. Emmenegger (Eds.), *Collective skill formation in the knowledge economy* (pp. 281–307). Oxford University Press.
Biermann, J. (2022). *Translating human rights in education: The influence of article 24 UN CRPD in Nigeria and Germany*. University of Michigan Press.
Biermann, J., & Powell, J. J. W. (2014). Institutionelle Dimensionen inklusiver Schulbildung: Herausforderungen der UN-Behindertenrechtskonvention für Deutschland, Island und Schweden im Vergleich. *Zeitschrift für Erziehungswissenschaften, 17*(4), 679–700.
Blanck, J. M. (2020). *Übergänge nach der Schule als "zweite Chance"?* Beltz Juventa.
Boli, J., Ramirez, F. O., & Meyer, J. W. (1985). Explaining the origins and expansion of mass education. *Comparative Education Review, 29*(2), 145–170.
European Agency for Special Needs and Inclusive Education. (2024). In P. Dráľ, A. Lenárt and A. Lecheval (Eds.), *European Agency Statistics on Inclusive Education: 2020/2021 School Year Dataset Cross-Country Report*. European Agency for Special Needs and Inclusive Education. https://www.european-agency.org/activities/data
European Parliament. (2017). *Inclusive education for learners with disabilities*. European Parliament.
Florian, L. (2019). On the necessary co-existence of special and inclusive education. *International Journal of Inclusive Education, 23*(7–8), 691–704. https://doi.org/10.1080/13603116.2019.1622801
Füssel, H.-P., & Kretschmann, R. (1993). *Gemeinsamer Unterricht für behinderte und nichtbehinderte Kinder*. Wehle.
Gomolla, M., & Radtke, F. O. (2002). *Institutionelle Diskriminierung*. Leske & Budrich.
Heidenheimer, A. J. (1997). *Disparate ladders: Why school policies differ in Germany, Japan, and Switzerland*. Transaction Publishers.
Heyer, K. (2021). What is a human right to inclusive education? The promises and limitations of the CRPD's inclusion mandate. In A. Köpfer, J. J. W. Powell, & R. Zahnd (Eds.), *International handbook of inclusive education* (pp. 45–57). Verlag Barbara Budrich.
Köpfer, A., Powell, J. J. W., & Zahnd, R. (Eds.). (2021). *International handbook of inclusive education: Global, national, and local perspectives*. Verlag Barbara Budrich.
Ludwig-Mayerhofer, W., Pollak, R., Solga, H., Menze, L., Leuze, K., & Edelstein, R., et al. (2019). Vocational education and training and transitions into the labor market. In H.P. Blossfeld & H.G. Roßbach (Eds.), *Education as a lifelong process* (3rd ed.). Springer.
Marshall, T. H. (1950). *Citizenship and social class and other essays*. Cambridge University Press.
Noesen, M. (in press, 2025). *Portfolioarbeit in der Grundschule: Ein Lernwerkzeug im Spannungsfeld zwischen Inklusion und Kompetenzstandardisierung*. Springer.
Pfahl, L. (2011). *Techniken der Behinderung*. Transcript Verlag.
Powell, J. J. W. (2006). Special education and the risk of becoming less educated. *European Societies, 8*(4), 577–599.
Powell, J. J. W. (2011/2016). *Barriers to inclusion: Special education in the United States and Germany*. Routledge.

Powell, J. J. W. (2020). Comparative education in an age of competition and collaboration. *Comparative Education, 56*(1), 57–78. https://doi.org/10.1080/03050068.2019.1701248

Powell, M. M. W. (2018). *Living at the heart of the UVA community*. KDP.

Powell, J. J. W., Edelstein, B., & Blanck, J. M. (2016). Awareness-raising, legitimation or backlash? Effects of the UN convention on the rights of persons with disabilities on education systems in Germany. *Globalisation, Societies and Education, 14*(2), 227–250.

Powell, J. J. W., Merz-Atalik, K., Ališauskienė, S., Brendel, M., Echeita, G., & Guðjónsdóttir, H., et al. (2019). Teaching diverse learners in Europe: Inspiring practices and lessons learned from Germany, Iceland, Lithuania, Luxembourg, Spain and Sweden. In Schuelka, M., C. Johnstone, G. Thomas, & A. Artiles (Eds.), *SAGE handbook of inclusion and diversity in education* (pp. 321–337). SAGE.

Ramberg, J., & Watkins, A. (2020). Exploring inclusive education across Europe: Some insights from the European agency statistics on inclusive education. *FIRE, 6*(1), 85–101. https://doi.org/10.32865/fire202061172

Richardson, J. G., & Powell, J. J. W. (2011). *Comparing special education: Origins to contemporary paradoxes*. Stanford University Press.

Solga, H. (2002). Stigmatization by negative selection: Explaining less-educated people's decreasing employment opportunities. *European Sociological Review, 18*(2), 159–178. https://doi.org/10.1093/esr/18.2.159

Stone, D. A. (1984). *The disabled state*. Temple University Press.

Taneja-Johansson, S., & Powell, J. J. W. (2024). Confronting the idealised 'Nordic model' in education with contemporary realities of special education in Sweden. *European Journal of Special Needs Education, 39*(6). https://doi.org/10.1080/08856257.2024.2425501

TdiverS Project (2024). Teaching diverse learners in school subjects. www.tdivers.eu

Thornton, P. H., Ocasio, W., & Lounsbury, M. (2012). *The institutional logics perspective*. Oxford University Press.

Tomlinson, S. (2017). *A sociology of special and inclusive education*. Routledge.

Tschanz, C., & Powell, J. J. W. (2020). Competing institutional logics and paradoxical universalism in disabled people's school-to-work transitions: Comparing Switzerland and the United States. *Social Inclusion, 8*(1), 155–167. https://doi.org/10.17645/si.v8i1.2373

UNESCO. (1994). *The Salamanca statement and framework for action on special needs education*. UNESCO.

UNESCO. (2020). Global Education Monitoring Report 2020. Inclusion and education: All means all. UNESCO.

UNESCO. (2022). A steady path forward: UNESCO 2022 report on public access to information. https://unesdoc.unesco.org/notice?id=p::usmarcdef_0000385479

United Nations. (2006). *UN convention on the rights of persons with disabilities*. United Nations.

United Nations. (2015). 2030 agenda for sustainable development. United Nations. http://www.un.org/sustainabledevelopment/development-agenda/

9
ARE WE PREPARING TEACHERS TO INCLUDE OR EXCLUDE?

Umesh Sharma

My conversation with Joanne Banks a couple of years ago made me reflect on my journey in the field of inclusive education. I must confess I have been highly sceptical of inclusive education and the possibility of it being a reality for all learners in the countries of the South and to some extent in the countries of the North as well. I am now convinced that inclusion is not only possible it could easily be achieved and could result in achieving both inclusion and excellence for all learners. However, it is not easy. One sector that has been a significant barrier in making this transformation a reality is teacher education. I have often asked the question: *is it possible that we have prepared teachers for exclusion and then we expect them to include all*? The research of many of our colleagues seems to suggest that teacher education, in most countries of the South, has not prepared teachers for inclusion (Ahsan, Sharma, & Deppeler, 2011; Loreman Sharma, Forlin, 2013; Sharma, Forlin, Deppeler, Yang, 2013). Unless we invest our energies to explore this question deeply, we will continue to do what we have done for many years, and we will continue to produce teachers who will not be able to make our classrooms inclusive.

It is important to highlight that reforming teacher education on its own may not fully address the problem, but it could make the task of making our school systems highly inclusive much easier across many countries. We will need to make sure that other aspects such as the formulation of better policies and resourcing of schools are also paid equal attention.

In this piece, I will first share the major drawbacks of our teacher education programs globally. I have had numerous opportunities to work on my own or with many of my colleagues in the countries of the North (the USA, Canada, Australia, Italy, Germany, and Switzerland) and the South (Bangladesh, India, China, Pakistan, Fiji, and Solomon Islands). My reflections are informed by our collective research and the work that we have done for various international agencies in these countries. I will then share possible ways we can address drawbacks.

Before sharing what's wrong with teacher education, let me first explain how I conceptualize inclusive education. There are many authors (Ainscow, Florian) whose work has influenced my thinking. I will always remain thankful to these colleagues who have truly made a difference in the field globally. It is important to confess that I have for a long time believed that inclusion was mainly about educating students with disabilities in regular schools. My conceptualization of the term was influenced by my tertiary education in India. I completed my undergraduate and post-graduate programs in special education in the 1990s. We learned that most students with disabilities could *only* be educated in special schools. We learned that in some countries, mainly the countries of the North, students with disabilities were being educated in regular schools. We used to often argue that inclusion cannot be successful in countries like India, Bangladesh, or Pakistan. It was largely an alien concept. I believe a major pessimism amongst many educators like myself was ingrained in the way we were educated and the key concepts like inclusion or inclusive education were defined and explained to us.

A complete transformation has taken place in how I view inclusion now. I define inclusion as 'an ongoing process involving the identification of barriers to learning and participation of all learners, including those with a range of diverse profiles. Inclusion is also about identifying context-sensitive and culturally responsive solutions to the barriers that many learners face. Additionally, implementing inclusive education is not possible in schools that fail to support educators with their inclusive education efforts' (Sharma & Subban, 2023, p. 105). We now know that inclusion is much more than just the placement of a student with a disability in a regular class/school. I believe that the best way for us to find out if a student is included could be determined when a learner, irrespective of any diversity, attends a school that their peers will attend, is accepted by everyone in the school, participates in the range of activities that a school offers, achieves in various curricular areas, has a sense of belonging to be part of the school, and feels happy to attend the school every day (Schwab et al., 2018). Most mainstream schools can achieve inclusion for all if we have robust policies that do not just articulate what needs to be done but also explain how it should be done and have provision for necessary resources to include all. We also need to have leaders who understand that inclusion is the best way to achieve excellence for all and ensure that educators are well-supported in implementing inclusive practices (Ainscow, 2016). We also need teachers who are well-equipped with their hearts, heads, and hands to include all (Sharma, 2018). The most difficult aspect of making our schools inclusive in most of the countries of the South remains ill-prepared teachers who lack an understanding of inclusion and how to make their classrooms inclusive (Sharma et al., 2013). It urgently requires us to reform teacher education.

Reforming teacher education is not easy, but without reforming teacher education, we will continue to struggle to create inclusive school systems in the countries of the South. Fixing the teacher education system will have a direct and wider impact on the new generation of teachers coming out of the university system. It will also indirectly and positively influence policymakers and school leaders because most policymakers and school leaders are often also products of the same tertiary education system that prepares teachers.

There are many aspects of teacher education systems in the countries of the South that have contributed towards the inadequate preparation of teachers to teach well in inclusive classrooms. I first discuss these issues and then provide possible ways for us to move forward.

- **Too much talk about theory.** We have done research looking at how teachers are being prepared to teach in inclusive classrooms across many countries (Sharma et al., 2013). The examination of the content of teacher education programs has consistently shown that teachers do learn about some theories, philosophical arguments, and some strategies but there are significant gaps in how teachers can apply this knowledge in real classrooms to include all learners. I have also seen that many teacher education programs cover content that makes teachers even more concerned about inclusion after they have finished their teacher education programs. For example, graduate teachers may learn about various disabling conditions, and characteristics of various disabilities, and, many may even learn to use checklists to identify 'disabled students' in their classrooms. We now know that this content could be counterproductive (Ainscow, 2016; Florian, 2017; Florian & Beaton, 2018) to the whole idea of inclusion. Rather than building teacher confidence to include all learners, teachers start feeling that they don't know enough about various disabling conditions and that they will not be able to teach all children, including those, about whom they have limited awareness. This could explain their higher degree of concern even when they have received some training in special education.
- **Misconception about inclusive education/inclusion.** Inclusion remains a very narrowly defined concept across the countries of the South. I have observed that inclusion and special education are seen as synonymous. Even policy and legislative documents in many of the countries where we have worked continue to reinforce the idea that inclusion is mainly about teaching students with special needs. Policies and legislative documents mandate/emphasize that students with disabilities be enrolled in regular schools but what happens after the enrolment remains unclear. There is a need for a significant shift in how we understand and conceptualize inclusion in local contexts.
- **Colonial approach to inclusion.** There is some reluctance about why and how inclusive practices be implemented in the countries of the South. Several authors, including myself, have written that the idea of 'inclusive education' originated in the West and has been imported to the countries of the East (or South). Policymakers, researchers, educators, and many other professionals like the idea of inclusion but remain sceptical about how it

can be implemented considering it is a foreign concept. Many textbooks adopted across universities in the countries of South are written by authors from Western countries.

- **Where are inclusive schools?** It is extremely important for teachers to apply the theory about inclusive education in real classroom settings. Graduate teachers often complete their teaching practice in schools where inclusive practices are almost non-existent. Consider a graduate teacher who has learned during their teacher training course that to include students with additional needs, the school must use a range of practices such as use cooperative learning, peer tutoring, and differentiated practices. However, graduate teachers rarely get opportunities to complete their teaching practicum in schools where such teaching practices are being used. On the contrary, they witness practices where students are often excluded because they learn differently. A very common practice in many of the schools that I have visited, I have seen students being grouped based on their abilities and taught together. For example, students in grade 7A are likely to have higher academic abilities compared to students in 7B, 7C, and so on. In a school with five 7th grade classrooms, students in 7E grade are likely to be those who are presumed to have the lowest abilities and/or additional needs. Clearly, when graduate teachers complete their teaching practice rounds in such schools where students of similar abilities are taught together, they are unlikely to be convinced that inclusion could be implemented in real classrooms. Mentor teachers in the placement schools are also not convinced themselves that inclusion is possible in their schools. Even they question the idea of inclusion. They will challenge the idea of inclusion. It is, therefore, not surprising that many graduate teachers return to university classrooms confused about implementing inclusive practices.

- **Teacher educators are not convinced.** Teacher educators are the product of the system where they have rarely witnessed inclusion in practice. They learn about inclusive education from textbooks written in the West or by local authors who have completed most of their tertiary education in the West. They teach about what, why, and how of inclusion often citing examples about how it is done in other countries. There remains a huge disconnect between theory and practice. So we need to ask this question: 'Are teacher educators confident and convinced that inclusion is possible in their respective countries'? There is not enough research on this topic. Some of the research that we have done in countries like Bangladesh (Ahsan et al., 2011) and the countries of the Pacific (Sharma et al., 2015, 2017) shows that while most teacher educators like the idea of inclusion, they are *not* convinced that it is possible for *all* children in the countries of the South. It is not surprising that when graduate teachers complete their teaching courses with these teacher educators, they may also like the idea but they also remain reluctant that schools could include learners with various diversities and abilities.

A way forward

In this chapter, I have presented a very disappointing picture of teacher education citing several examples of what has contributed towards the formation of this gloomy picture. The readers must be wondering if everything I have written so far is true then '*is it really possible for us to prepare our teachers to include all learners*'? Having worked in many countries of the Global South (e.g. India, Bangladesh, China, Pakistan, Solomon Islands, and Fiji), I am convinced that it is possible. We need to understand that it will take some time and it will not be easy. However, if we are committed to making the change, we can transform our teacher education programs and will be able to prepare teachers who are ready to teach with their hearts, heads, and hands (Sharma, 2018). I identify five key principles that should form the foundation of reforming the teacher education systems in the countries of the South. The principles are also relevant for most teacher education programs globally.

Principle one: Building upon the strengths of the system

Teacher educators must delve into exploring local, traditional, and historical practices that have fostered inclusion within their respective contexts or countries. Throughout my experiences in various countries, I've encountered numerous traditional, historical, and religious practices that have championed the notion of inclusion. Many scholars, including myself, have discussed how religion can profoundly influence the transformation of our educational institutions to embrace marginalized learners and make our schools and society more inclusive. For instance, British scholar Miles (1995) identified several practices utilized across South Asia to educate learners with disabilities long before similar endeavours elsewhere. He highlighted adaptations in curricula and teaching materials dating back 2000 years, evidenced by artifacts discovered in Taxila in India. Additionally, scholars like Singh (2001) have documented the ancient 'Gurukul' system in India, which tailored education to students' diverse cultural, social, and economic backgrounds, emphasizing life skills development for each individual. The teacher, in the Gurukul system, was responsible for modifying the content if a student was having any difficulties in accessing or understanding the content. The teacher also used community resources and educated all children in their natural environment.

Miles (1995) also observed in Pakistan a propensity to adopt beneficial practices from Muslim history rather than merely emulating Western innovations, citing examples like vaccination. This utilization of religion to promote certain practices, sometimes termed as 'pious fraud', suggests that even if inconsistent from a rationalist perspective, leveraging religious influence for advancing inclusion should be considered. In my previous research (Sharma, 2011), I examined the teachings of Islamic scholars such as Bazna and Hatab (2005), revealing Quranic injunctions to respect individual differences and include people with disabilities in society.

The Quranic analysis further underscores the view that excluding individuals due to disabilities is considered sinful in Islam. Instead, Islam advocates for respect, acceptance, and education for individuals with disabilities, viewing them as gifts from Allah that should be nurtured with available knowledge and resources. Disregarding this guidance would be deemed a rejection of the divine assistance mercifully provided by Allah. These practices need to form the foundation of teacher education courses. The graduate teachers need to learn that the idea of inclusion may have come from Western countries, but there were strong roots to this idea within their own context/countries.

Principle two: It takes a village, then teach graduates to live and work like villagers

Graduate teachers in most countries learn to teach on their own. They rarely get opportunities to team teach and learn about collaborating with other teachers, parents, and professionals. Teaching in an inclusive classroom is difficult, if not impossible, if the school community makes collective efforts. In countries and contexts where resources are limited, the need to find and use existing resources effectively is critical. Graduate teachers need to learn how they will be able to work collaboratively with other school personnel to include all learners. This should become a core competency for all graduate teachers. The idea of collaborating and working in teams also aligns well with the traditional practices of many countries in South Asia and the Pacific (Sharma, 2020).

In our multinational research project (Sharma et al., 2023), we found that high efficacy in collaboration was one of the top predictors of in-service teachers' intention to use teaching practices. An inclusive classroom is like a village. When all villagers work together and support each other, they create a culture where people are ready to support each other. They do it not because they have to do it, they do it because that's what villagers do in a traditional village. They support each other and make sure that no one is overburdened with the responsibility of looking after one child. They are jointly responsible for all members of their community.

Principle three: Keep it simple

I have observed that we have made inclusion unnecessarily complex in teacher education programs. A key focus of programs across most teacher education programs is often covering information about various disabilities, characteristics of children with various disabilities, and the use of checklists to identify students with disabilities (Sharma et al., 2013). Graduate teachers are overwhelmed with the information presented and often start feeling more concerned about inclusion. Research by many of our colleagues has shown that there is no special education pedagogy (Davis & Florian, 2004; Florian, 2017). Good teaching is good teaching. Inclusive teachers apply good teaching methods more frequently and intensively to teach all learners. Rather than focussing on various disabilities, the focus of any inclusive education courses should be on demystifying popular assumptions. The content of any inclusive education teacher education courses should be simple. It could cover topics such as 'understanding the learner'; 'strategies to motivate and engage all learners'; 'methods to assess the impact of teaching'; group teaching strategies such as peer tutoring, cooperative learning, and differentiated instruction; collaborating with parents/carers and other professionals; and, modifying assessment and curriculum content. This content may be covered in one or more than one subject. It is important that all teacher educators take joint responsibility and make connections with the content they teach so that graduate teachers learn that inclusion is not something we do for some children, we do it for all children.

Principle four: Begin inclusion for students who are already in our classrooms

Pre-service teachers often learn that inclusion means that we need to include a student who may have difficulties in one or more areas. I believe this is problematic. Pre-service teachers need to learn that they will struggle to implement inclusive practices, as well as to teach well, if they are not competent to include students who are already in our schools. They need to learn about what they can do to ensure that the classrooms are highly engaging for all learners who are in our schools. In other words, they need to be highly competent in using teaching practices that are effective for learners who do not require any significant adjustments in teaching. Pre-service teachers in these classrooms will learn to be competent to use high-impact teaching strategies that engage all learners, enhance their academic excellence and prevent any challenging behaviours. Some of the teaching strategies that they need to learn to create engaging classrooms for all learners will include using cooperative or collaborative learning strategies, universal design for learning strategies, differentiated instructions, effective feedback, team teaching, and, collaborating with paraprofessionals and parents. When pre-service teachers learn to use some of these high-impact teaching practices, the inclusion of students who need additional support will become easier. Unless the use of highly effective teaching practices becomes a norm in our classrooms, pre-service (and in-service) teachers will struggle to include all learners and continue to blame students for the failure of inclusion.

Principle five: Consider using student and parent/carer voices

One of the most powerful ways to transform our schooling system in the countries of the South is to ensure that teachers start using student (Schwab et al., 2018) and parent voices/feedback (Sharma et al., 2022) to change teaching practices. However, it is not easy to bring about this change in many countries of the South. Seeking student feedback is not common in most, if not all, countries of the South. Students have a much lower status in schools and their voices are not considered important. The shift in thinking that student voices can be an effective tool to change teaching practices can only occur when teachers realize that it benefits them in some way. It will also require strong encouragement by school leaders and policymakers to use student voice. Schools could be encouraged to share the views of the students about how they wish to learn and report to teachers how the use of the student voice was used to make adjustments to their teaching. We used similar ideas in a large project in Bangladesh. At the end of the school day, students were asked to report three things: 'what they liked about the day', 'what they didn't like about the day' and 'suggest one change that the school/teacher could make to make their classrooms more engaging/interesting'. The students provided this information anonymously to their respective schools. Teachers worked in small teams to look at the student data and made adjustments to their teaching activities. Within a short time, a significant shift was noticed and student engagement across all participating schools increased dramatically. Similar data can also be collected from parents about the education of their children. The data from students and parents could provide new ways to transform school culture. Teacher educators could design university assignments that require pre-service students to seek feedback from the students they teach and document any changes that pre-service teachers make to their teaching as a result of the feedback received. Assignments of this nature will ensure that the classrooms and schools become more inclusive of all learners by ensuring that student voices are instrumental in transforming the classroom/schooling culture.

Conclusion

In conclusion, the journey towards inclusive education is both challenging and imperative. Reflecting on personal scepticism and global observations, it is evident that the transformation of our educational systems hinges significantly on reforming teacher education. While acknowledging the complexities and barriers, it is essential to underscore the potential for achieving inclusion and excellence for all learners.

The identified drawbacks in teacher education programs globally, ranging from theoretical emphasis to misconceptions about inclusion, colonial legacies, lack of exposure to inclusive practices, and teacher educators' own uncertainties, paint a daunting picture. However, amidst these challenges lies an opportunity for reform.

Five key principles emerge as foundational pillars for transforming teacher education systems worldwide:

1 **Building upon strengths:** Leveraging local, traditional, and historical practices that foster inclusion within respective contexts, acknowledging diverse religious and cultural influences.
2 **Collective collaboration:** Shifting from isolated teaching approaches to collaborative models that emulate the supportive dynamics of a village, where stakeholders work collectively towards inclusion.

3 **Simplicity in approach:** Streamlining inclusive education content to focus on fundamental principles of effective teaching rather than overwhelming with complex disability-related information.
4 **Inclusion as a norm:** Prioritizing effective teaching practices that engage all learners, laying the groundwork for seamless inclusion of students with additional needs.
5 **Student and parent/carer voices:** Acknowledging the transformative power of student and parent feedback in shaping teaching practices and fostering a culture of inclusion.

While these principles offer a pathway forward, implementing them requires a collective commitment and sustained effort. It involves a paradigm shift in how we perceive, prepare, and support teachers in their journey towards inclusive education. However, the potential rewards—creating equitable, supportive, and engaging learning environments for all learners—justify the endeavour.

In the pursuit of inclusive education, teacher education stands as a linchpin. By addressing its shortcomings and embracing transformative principles, we can pave the way for inclusive schooling systems that empower every learner to thrive, regardless of their background or abilities. Through concerted action, dedication, and a shared vision of inclusion, we can chart a course towards educational excellence for all.

References

Ahsan, M., Sharma, U., & Deppeler, J. (2011). Beliefs of pre-service teacher education institutional heads about inclusive education in Bangladesh. *Bangladesh Education Journal*, *10*(1), 9–29.
Ainscow, M. (2016). *Struggles for equity in education: The selected works of Mel Ainscow*. Routledge World Library of Educationalists Series.
Bazna, M. S., & Hatab, T. A. (2005). Disability in the Qur'an'. *Journal of Religion, Disability & Health*, *9*(1), 5–27.
Davis, P., & Florian, L. (2004). *Teaching Strategies and Approaches for Children with Special Educational Needs, A scoping study [Research Report 516]* DfES
Florian, L. (2017). The concept of inclusive pedagogy. In G. Hallett & F. Hallett (Eds.), *Transforming the role of the SENCO* (2nd ed., pp. 130–141). Open University Press.
Florian, L., & Beaton, M. (2018). Inclusive pedagogy in action: Getting it right for every child. *International Journal of Inclusive Education*, *22*(8), 870–884. https://www.tandfonline.com/doi/full/10.1080/13603116.2017.1412513
Loreman, T., Sharma, U., & Forlin, C. (2013). Do pre-service teachers feel ready to teach in inclusive classrooms: A four country study of teaching efficacy. *Australian Journal of Teacher Education*, *38*(1), article 3. Available at: http://ro.ecu.edu.au/cgi/viewcontent.cgi?article=1988&context=ajte
Miles, M. (1995). Disability in an Eastern religious context: Historical perspectives. *Disability and Society*, *10*(1), 49–69.
Schwab, S., Sharma, U., & Loreman, T. (2018). Are we included? Secondary Students' perception of inclusion climate in their schools. *Teacher and Teaching Education*, *75*, 30–39.

Sharma, U. (2011). Teaching in inclusive classrooms: Changing heart, head and hands. *Bangladesh Education Journal*, *10*(2), 7–18.

Sharma, U. (2018). Preparing to Teach in Inclusive Classrooms. *Oxford Research Encyclopedia of Education.* Retrieved August 26, 2019, from https://oxfordre.com/education/view/10.1093/acrefore/9780190264093.001.0001/acrefore-9780190264093-e-113

Sharma, U. (2020). Inclusive education in the Pacific: challenges and opportunities. *Prospects*. https://doi.org/10.1007/s11125-020-09498-7

Sharma, U., Forlin, C., Deppeler, J., & Yang, G. (2013). Reforming teacher education for inclusion in developing countries in the Asia Pacific region. *Asian Journal of Inclusive Education*, *1*(1), 3–16.

Sharma, U., Loreman, T., May, F., Romano, A., Lozano, C., Avramidis, E., Woodcock, S., Subban, P., & Kullmann, H. (2023). Measuring collective efficacy for inclusion in a global context. *European Journal of Special Needs Education*. https://doi.org/10.1080/08856257.2023.2195075

Sharma, U., Loreman, T., & Simi, J. (2017). Stakeholder perspectives on barriers and facilitators of inclusive education in the Solomon Islands. *Journal of Research in Special Educational Needs*, *17*(2), 141–151. https://doi.org/10.1111/1471-3802.12375

Sharma, U., Simi, J., & Forlin, C. (2015). Preparedness of pre-service teachers for inclusive education in the Solomon Islands, *Australian Journal of Teacher Education*, *40*(5), 103–116.

Sharma, U., & Subban, P. (2023). Utilising a global social justice lens to explore indicators of inclusive educators. In Tierney, R.J, Rizviv, F., Erkican, K. (Eds.), *International encyclopedia of education* (4th ed., pp. 104–114). https://doi.org/10.1016/B978-0-12-818630-5.12053-6

Sharma, U., Woodcock, S., May, F., & Subban, P. (2022). Examining parental perception of inclusive education climate. *Frontiers in Education*, *7*, 907742. https://doi.org/10.3389/feduc.2022.907742

Singh, R. (2001, February). Need of the hour- A paradigm shift in education. Paper presented at the North-South Dialogue on Inclusive Education, Mumbai, India.

10
REINVENTING THE SQUARE WHEEL

The past and future of special and alternative education

Sally Tomlinson

Introduction

> Never forget the past: you may need it again in the future

The wheels of a mainstream schooling system that developed over two centuries in England were always a bit wobbly, and the wheel that took care of those removed into separate provisions was positively square and never worked well. The spokes that held the wheel together, over the years dropped off, or were renamed, thus the idiots, imbeciles, feeble-minded, educable defectives, paupers, delinquent children, all those who in the 19th century who might be a drain on the country's finances, turned by the 21st century into around two million children and young people with myriad 'special educational needs', disabilities and disruptive behaviours, who needed school support, special schools, units, resources, alternative provision, secure schools and more. This second system also needed an expanding number of professionals to discover, assess, diagnose, treat, teach, and care for the special and disabled, either employed in state bureaucracies or as private experts. The government fears that all these children, young people and the experts might be a drain on central and local finances have been amply realised, as by 2023 local authorities in England were apparently some £2.3 billion in debt for SEND and AP services (Hall, 2023). Of this, apparently some £1.3 billion had been spent on private provision (Booth, 2024) government having come full circle back to the late 18th and 19th centuries when private enterprise and business paid to open schools for the 'indigent Blind', deaf and dumb, and the Misses White opened their private school for idiots in Bath (Pritchard, 1963).

120 Conversations and Key Debates on Inclusive and Special Education

I came into this dual system in the 1970s, teaching in a primary school and then a teacher training College, and wondering why an increasing number of children were being assessed and placed in special schools – the majority in the disgracefully named schools for the educationally subnormal (ESN). It was clear that most of these children were from manual or semi-skilled working-class families, with many children from newly arrived migrant families placed in ESN schools before much of a chance to settle in mainstream schools. It was also obvious that special education as a sub-system of mainstream state schooling was expanding post-war, from the 8% of children envisaged as needing 'special educational treatment in special schools or elsewhere' falling into 11 (then 10) categories of 'handicap', to 20% by the time the Committee chaired by Mary Warnock reported in 1978. As many more labels and categories had been created or suggested, the Warnock report used the title of Birmingham Professor Ron Gulliford's 1971 book *Special Educational Needs* to describe the variety of children and young people who were candidates for this sub-system, by 2024 really a whole second 'schooling' system. From starting to research the question of why and how children were labelled as ESN for my own PhD I have spent years writing and teaching about educational policy, especially special, inclusive and exclusive education, and the place of Black and minority children in the system (Tomlinson, 1981/2019, 2021). On 20 May 2021, over forty years after my ESN research, I took part in a BBC TV programme on the 'disgraceful 1 labelling' in a programme made on ESN schools by producer Lytannia Shannon and Director Steve McQueen, in which adults who had been sent to these schools wept as they recalled their non-education. This was followed up two years later by a meeting in the House of Commons where reparations for those who had suffered were discussed. This chapter briefly touches on the history and developments in special education to the present day from my perspective.

In the olden days

Fiction writer Malcom Bradbury was right to point out the importance of understanding the past in order to make sense of current and likely future events. Studying the history, it is clear that the most important issue in the special and alternative education system, (with later exceptions) was that it has mainly always been a mechanism for the social and economic control of the lower classes in the persistent British social class hierarchy. This was largely due to early fears from the 18th century that the disabled and defective lower classes might not be able to work, be a drain on local authorities deemed under Poor Laws to be responsible for them and might turn to criminal behaviour. Interest in these groups intensified as the industrial revolution evolved, in which many more workers were needed for factories in urban areas. The Chair of the Commission on the Blind, Deaf, Dumb and Others, Lord Egerton, whose family had made money from the West Indian sugar trade and slavery, was concerned that these unfortunates 'if left uneducated, become a burden to themselves and a weighty burden to the state' and might ultimately create a 'great torrent of pauperism' (Report of the Royal Commission on the Blind, Deaf, Dumb and others in the United Kingdom, 1889). The remedy was a proliferation of both state and private 'Asylums' (the Lancaster Asylum charging over 50 guineas per annum), workhouses, where as many inmates as possible were set to work, and the removal of defective and troublesome children from elementary schools into special classes, and schools and their training for manual, moral and domestic work. This last was important, as a category of 'moral imbecile' was created in 1913, which was mainly unmarried young women who had babies, girls in domestic service being especially at risk from the attentions of their 'masters'.

By the early 20th century, the largest group of defectives, described in a 1908 report as the feeble-minded (Report of the Royal Commission on the Care and Control of the Feeble-minded, 1908) became the educable defectives, then the ESN, then children with learning and behaviour difficulties and eventually those with behavioural, social, emotional and mental health problems. Children with physical and sensory disabilities, and the 'mental defectives', (those not even considered 'educable' until a 1970 Act), were catered for in both state and private institutions, and the schooling system struggled to accommodate increasing numbers of children who could not or would not conform to the practices of what passed for mass normal education. Even in the early days, it was stressed that special provisions should not be too expensive. In 1899, the Chancellor of the Exchequer himself expressed anxiety that local authorities 'especially in Ireland' would 'discover' too many defective children in need of special schooling.

It was always the case that the middle and upper classes also produced 'defective' children, but they were usually able to provide privately for them. The late Queen Elizabeth's grandmother Queen Mary, gave birth to John, a child with epilepsy and learning problems, who was isolated from the royal family and died aged 13. Worcester College for the Blind in 1866 promised to 'ensure that blind children of opulent parents might obtain an education suitable to their station in life'. Medical man and author R. Tredgold wrote a best-selling book on *Mental Deficiency* in 1908, in which he noted that there were in the country 'hundreds of feeble-minded persons, many of them gentle folk by birth', they could apparently perform simple house tasks, have hobbies and 'enter into the social amusements of their class' (Tredgold, 1908) but Tredgold was a confirmed eugenicists and was convinced that 'the bulk of primary defectives come from psychopathic stock', who were from lower social classes.

By the end of the 19th century, a variety of interests were being served by the development of state special education provision. Medical doctors claimed new methods of 'diagnosis', the developing professions of psychologists and psychiatrists used new tests (especially for IQ), and charities and religious groups claimed humanitarian interests. Special schools emphasised manual and trade training and served economic interests, moving 'defective' children out of mainstream schools ensured that such children did not take up teacher time and interfere with preparing 'normal' children for tests. Costs in all provision, from workhouses to special schools to occupational centres run by local Mental Deficiency Committees were kept as low as possible. Political interests were served by these placements in separate schools and institutions, given the assumed links between defect, unemployment and potential crime. I wrote in 1982 that the social origins of special education could be traced to this separation of the defective and troublesome, and thus special education could be regarded as a 'safety valve' allowing for the smoother development of 'normal' schooling (Tomlinson, 1982). It was probably a coincidence that the Department for Education in 2020 called a project to reduce local authority spending on SEND a 'Safety Valve' programme.

Into the 20th century

Children and young people from lower social classes continued during the early 20th century to be placed in stigmatised kinds of provision, avoided by the middle classes. There was more segregation of defective children as the influence of the eugenics movement led to political fears that such children were a danger to society, linked to moral depravity, crime, pauperism, prostitution and unemployment. The report in 1908 of the Royal Commission on the Care and Control of the Feeble-minded had much influence on the future segregation of defective children, singling out working class parents for condemnation, and blaming these parents and families for their children's social and educational deficiencies, a view which has persisted over the years (Royal Commission on the Care and Control of the feeble-Minded, 1908). I sat in the basement of the Bodleian library in Oxford and read all eight volumes of this report, being both amused and angered by it. Counting the number of feeble-minded in communities was carried out by some dubious research methods, putting advertisements in local newspapers urging people to name those they regarded as feeble-minded, for example. People wrote in nominating their relatives! After 1914 local education authorities retained control of most defective children and could force parents to send their children into special schooling via a 'certification' process, which did nothing to reduce the stigma of special schooling. Meanwhile in the UK as in other Western countries, special school teachers claimed competence in dealing with the children, a mental testing movement helped along psychological interests and academics claimed interest in developing 'intelligence' testing and placement of children. In the 1920s and 1930s Professor Cyril Burt had much influence on standardising tests and influencing selective education policies, despite his work eventually being regarded as fraudulent. I studied sociology at Liverpool University where Burt had his first academic job and attended lectures by his biographer Leslie Henshaw, a Professor at Liverpool until the 1970s. I was particularly impressed by the information that Burt thanked his landladies for ironing his trousers!, not so much by his condemnation of the 'dull and backward' (Hearnshaw, 1979).

Although critical sociological views on special education have never been popular, when I began to study the history and developments, it was clear that medical, psychological, educational and political interests were served by an expansion of special schooling and placements, especially after 1945, when 'Handicapped Pupil' forms were required in the bureaucracy and HP1, signed by a medical doctor could compel parents to send their children into special education. Other professional interests expanded, as more children behaving badly in ordinary schools were discovered and a short-lived category of maladjusted was created, with a Committee on Maladjusted Children recommending an integrated service in which medical, psychological, psychiatric, social workers, speech therapists and others to be involved. Cyril Burt's first book on young people had been *The Young Delinquent*, and the care and control of those who had actually broken the law remained closely bound up with those non-criminal children regarded as badly behaved and in need of special schooling.

The ESN label was applied to more children, two-thirds of referrals of 'handicapped' children in the 1960s being candidates for this category – teachers being understandably keen to have troublesome children with both learning and behaviour issues removed from 'normal' classrooms. The Warnock report noted that the 'needs of the ESN remained obstinately unsatisfied despite continuous expansion since 1945' (Warnock, 1978). The label had become ESN (M-mild or moderate) and ESN-S (severe) after a 1970 Act brought all 'handicapped' children under educational control. There was continued interest in the expansion of categories of handicap, a conference in London in 1966 noting the dyslexic child (difficulty with the printed word), aphasia (children not deaf but with communication problem, the autistic child, (those apparently 'unable to tune in to ordinary human wavelengths'), the psychiatrically crippled child (stressed by social conditions) and the socially handicapped child (poor children). The Warnock report, deploring the stigma attached to special schooling and recommending the abolition of statutory categories, suggested, on the basis of two research studies in London and the Isle of Wight, that labels be abolished and some 20% of children be regarded as having special educational needs, catered for in both ordinary schools and special schools, units and centres. This report continued the tradition of blaming poorer families for their children's educational issues writing that 'We are fully aware that many children with educational difficulties may suffer from familial or wider social deficiencies (they) show educational difficulties because they do not obtain from their families the quality of stimulation or sense of stability which is necessary for proper educational progress' (Warnock, 1979, p. 4). Instead of focusing on problems of poverty, poor housing and health, a proliferation of Associations, Institutions and Centres, accompanied with an expanding number of professionals devoted to working with children in various non-statutory categories has developed over the years, with state, private and charitable finance.

By the 1970s, parents of Caribbean origin were especially angry that Black children were over-represented in ESN schooling and also in maladjusted and EBD

(Emotional and Behavioural Disturbed) provision. New types of provision for poor school behaviour became popular with 'normal' schools and teachers who continued to refer increasing numbers of poor and minority children into separate provision. Behavioural Centres, known as Pupil Referral Units (PRUs) (DES, 1978) were set up in local authorities, 239 in 63 areas by 1979, plus other centres for disruptive children, a 'multitude of sin-bins' according to two academics Berger and Mitchell (1978). Drugs were often prescribed to keep children quiet, as I observed on my research visits to special schools and units, one Headteacher of a special school noting a boy asleep on the floor and commenting 'Thank heaven for Valium'. The over-representation of Black, other minority and working-class white children in varieties of exclusion from mainstream schooling has continued into the 21st century.

The deficit industry

Studying, researching and teaching about special education over the years led me to write an article in 1985 on *The expansion of special education* and another in 2012 on *The Irresistible rise of the SEN* industry (Tomlinson, 1985) in which I tried to explain in measured academic terms the anger and disgust I felt that a society that claimed to be civilised had developed and continued to run an education system that devalued so many of its children, regarding them as so deficient they could not join in schooling with the rest of their peers despite national and international moves toward 'inclusive 'schooling. Observing in schools and other institutions and reading social histories of the treatment of 'defectives' who became those with the main special educational needs raised serious questions about the power and influence of elite groups. Committees and commissions on the 'special' always seemed to be Chaired by Lords, Ladies, or religious and charitable men, Mrs Warnock becoming Lady Warnock after her Chairing duties. Politicians and increasing numbers of professionals also had vested interests in claims to be 'doing good' to the less fortunate. While I termed this 'benevolent humanitarianism' in 1982, John Richardson and his colleagues probably were right to describe it as 'punitive benevolence (Richardson & Powell, 2011). Despite more acceptance over the years of learning difficulties and disabilities – the Disability movement from the 1970s helping this along – there has been no genuine acceptance of difference and disabilities in education, especially for poorer children and young people. We should stop using the weasel words of 'disadvantage' and 'deprivation'. The majority of families taking 'benefits' and with children with special educational needs are actually in work, often in more than one low-paid job.

'Needs' has been a contested term over the years. Scotland was a kinder country in which to have 'additional needs 'and Finland would offer 'educational support' to some 30% of young people without any stigma. But a large literature in England continued to spell out the need for educational, political, private and charitable organisations to rescue the degenerates and defectives for the good of the whole society, especially through separate educational provisions. Prime Minister Thatcher's friend Sir Keith Joseph, oversaw a short-lived programme for the 40% of children he considered to be lower attainers in the 1980s. Another keen follower Sir Ian Duncan-Smith set up a curiously named Centre for Social Justice which from 2004 produced papers such as *Breakdown Britian*, which blamed family breakdown, economic dependence (unemployment) educational failure, debt, drug and alcohol addiction for the problems the poor caused in society. Advances in neuroscience were repeating (eugenic) genetic and hereditarian explanations for social problems. Blaming 'deprived brains' for low educational attainments and other problems was becoming popular by the 2000s. The Cabinet Office in 2008 produced a paper on social mobility which included pictures of two brain scans purporting to be of a 'normal' child's brain and a shrivelled brain due to maternal neglect (Cabinet Office, 2008; Centre for Social Justice, 2006). Later reports and papers reproduced these scans, which were actually from two children, the smaller brain actually being that of a totally neglected child from a Romanian orphanage during the cruel Ceausescu regime (Perry, 2002). A popular text on special education by Frederickson and Cline in 2000 reproduced a scan which claimed to show the brain of a dyslexic child versus a 'normal' readers brain! (Frederickson & Cline, 2009). A 'deficit industry' dealing with nearly a third of all children and young people still treated as sub-standard humans into the 21st century is now supported by the expanded psychological and psychiatric and other professions claiming the ability to assess and treat what is now described as the neurodiversity of many of these children.

Middle-class interests

From the 1980s the 'needs of' middle and aspirant parents who had more knowledge of the system, especially in England and the USA, led to an expansion of the SEND industry (Disability added to SEN via a 1995 Act). Up to this time, middle-class parents developed strategies to avoid their children being give labels with a stigma- dull, remedial, subnormal, maladjusted. Physical or sensory disabilities were acceptable and education in both private and state maintained special schools for these conditions was always acceptable. Class interests changed when local authority multi-professional teams post-Warnock decided on placements and resources with 'Statements' needed for many of these resources and a code of practice led to more parental claims. A judgment in 1982 that Local authorities should pay for private provision encouraged demand for private places and services. A Conservative agenda notionally offering parents 'choice' in schooling and to act as vigilantes if they felt their needs were not met, plus an increasingly competitive, test-oriented mainstream schooling, led more middle-class parents to claim resources for their children's special needs. Litigation became common, with law firms offering their services, and special Tribunals were needed to mitigate conflicts. Local authorities, despite having legal duties to provide school places and resources, were never given enough money for expanded claims, and in turn developed strategies to deny or slow the assessment process. In the USA, academics had noted the ways in which stigmatised categories could become respectable if filled by middle-class children. Thus, dyslexia and autism, first legally recognised in England via a 1970 Chronically Sick and Disabled Persons Act, and ADHD – Attention Deficit Hyperactive Disorder, became respectable categories to be claimed by parents and many 'celebrities' in their memoirs. When interviewing administrators in both England and the USA for research on lower attainers a frequent comment was that 'middle class parents want their children to be given labels of autistic spectrum disorder, autism, or ADHD'. Those with Oppositional Conduct Disorder (OCD) and other labels for behavioural issues were likely to be working class and minority children in both countries (Tomlinson, 2017). I certainly found the 'medicalisation of behaviour' was common and political interest in claims for 'neurodiversity' in children was increasingly used to explain learning and behavioural issues. In the USA academics were exploring the category manipulation through which formally stigmatised labels were taken over by middle-class parents, which especially affected racially minority families who were still left with fewer resources and access to 'good' schools' (Saatcioglu & Skrtic, 2019).

Fixing the broken wheel

The 2014 Education Act and a subsequent 3rd Code of practice for SEND in England in 2015 cemented the financial crisis which overtook the SEND industry. The creation of Academy schools in 2002, with schools encouraged to link in multi-academy trusts (MATS), and the creation of 'Free' schools from 2010, encouraged the setting up of expensive tax-payer funded 'Free' special schools. More parents were concerned that their children could not learn in the competitive exam-oriented orientation of school and welcomed an Act that changed Statements to Education, Health and Care Plans (EHCP) to children and young people 0–25. The 2014 Act notionally gave parents some control over resources if their child was given a Plan, which actually led to more claims and litigation for resources and placements as local authorities were even shorter of money for increased demand. The duty to pay for private provision meant that private providers were making profits from tax-payers. In addition, children's services faced budget cuts, children were increasingly being excluded from schools for unacceptable behaviour and placed in Alternative Provision, usually renamed PRUs, now subject to their own legal requirements.

The government finally realised that this developing SEND and AP system was in chaos and set up a review body in 2019 which reported in March 2022 followed by a *Special needs and Alternative Provision Improvement Plan* (Department of Education, 2022, 2023) a year later. Government was particularly unstable in this period and there were three Education Secretaries of State for England and Wales between the review and the improvement plan, but a further publication in 2023 set out a 'road map' for local authorities to follow. The review noted that there were nearly one and a half million children identified with some form of SEND, and 87% of those in existing alternative provision had some form of special educational need-especially 'social, emotional and mental health needs', a mental health crisis having been acknowledged after the Covid-19 pandemic and its continuing effects. More children were being excluded from schools on a temporary or permanent basis and more were refusing to attend or whose parents had lost faith in schooling. The main proposal in the review report was for a single national SEND and Alternative Provision system, with national standards for any provision offered, and accountability for money spent and resources provided. In effect, this was to be funding for a separate education system for over 25% of young people in the country, with a large part of the money going to private providers making profits. One Abu Dhabi investment fund was making money running private SEND schools and one tax haven registered a Director paid over a million per annum. Attempts are to reduce budgets all round, especially for the 'high needs' category which has the most children in private provision, including paying private consultancies to help local authorities produce local reforms. One outcome is intended to be the placement of more responsibility on mainstream schools for the very children they have historically been keen to see removed. It seems unlikely that mainstream schools, parents or the young people themselves, will be happy with the suggested new arrangements.

The challenge for those in power is to make sense of the consequences of previous policies and try to avoid the mistakes, deliberate or otherwise of the past. Knowledge of the consequences of segregating children from each other already exists. Knowledge of the poorer life prospects of those who have been in stigmatised forms of special education already exists. Requiring teachers in mainstream to 'include' more children but without the money, resources, or training, but holding them accountable if outcomes for the children are not good will lead to more anger and confusion In an education system which sustains inequalities. Schools, their teachers and other professionals may find themselves continuing to maintain this inequality. Paying consultants to change systems they have never worked in has never been a good idea. A developing second education system based on the deficit views of young people is not guaranteed to improve their life chances or make for a cohesive democratic society.[1]

Note

1 This chapter is part of Tomlinson's current research in progress on "*Special needs and sin-bins*".

References

Berger, P., & Mitchell, G. (1978). *A mulitude of sin-bins*. The Times Educational Supplement, 7th July.

Booth, S. (2024). How investors are making millions from the bankrupt SEND system. *Schools Week*, December 15.
Cabinet Office. (2008). *Getting on, getting ahead: A discussion paper analysing) trends and drivers of social mobility*. Cabinet Office Strategy Unit.
Centre for Social Justice. (2006). *Breakdown Britain*. Centre for Social Justice.
Department of Education. (2022). *Right support, right place, right time: Government consultation on special educational needs and alternative provision*. DfE.
Department of Education. (2023). *Special educational needs (SEND) and alternative provision (AP) improvement plan*. DfE.
Department of Education and Science. (1978). *Behavioural units: A survey of special units for pupils with behaviour problems*. Department of Education and Science.
Frederickson, N., & Cline, T. (2009). *Special educational needs: Inclusion and diversity Maidenhead*. Open University Press.
Hall, R. (2023). "Funding black hole: Councils grapple with 'catastrophic' debt for SEN children" *The Guardian*, January 28.
Hearnshaw, L. S. (1979). Cyril Burt. *Psychologist*. Hodder and Stoughton
Perry, F. (2002). Childhood experience and the expression of genetic potential: What childhood experience tells us about nature and nurture. *Brain and Mind, 3*, 79–100.
Pritchard, R. (1963). *Education of the handicapped 1769-1960*. Routledge and Kegan Paul.
Report of the Royal Commission on the Blind, Deaf, Dumb and others in the United Kingdom. (1889). The Egerton report. HMSO.
Report of the Royal Commission on the Care and Control of the Feeble-minded. (1908). HMSO (eight volumes).
Richardson, J. G., & Powell, J. W. (2011). *Comparing special education: From origins to contemporary paradoxes Stanford*. Stanford University Press.
Saatcioglu, A., & Skrtic, T. M. (2019). Categorisation by organisational manipulation of categories in a racially desegregated school system. *American Journal of Sociology, 125*(1), 184–260.
Tomlinson, S. (1981/2019). *Educational sub normality, a study in decision-making*. London: Routledge (re-issued 2019 in the Routledge Library Editions: special educational needs. no 55).
Tomlinson, S. (1982). *A sociology of special education* (p. 45). Routledge and Kegan Paul.
Tomlinson, S. (1985). The expansion of special education. *Oxford Review of Education, 2*(2), 195–205.
Tomlinson, S. (2012). The irresistible rise of the SEN industry. *Oxford Review of Education, 38*(3), 267–286.
Tomlinson, S. (2017). *A sociology of special and inclusive education*. Routledge.
Tomlinson, S. (2021). Disgraceful Labelling: Race, special education and exclusion. Blog for Exclusion project. Department of Education, University of Oxford.
Tredgold, A. F. (1908). *Mental deficiency* (1st edition-9 editions following). Bailliere Tindall and Cox.
Warnock, H. M. (1978). *Report of the committee of enquiry into the education of handicapped children and young people*. https://webarchive.nationalarchives.gov.uk/ukgwa/20101007182820/http:/sen.ttrb.ac.uk/attachments/21739b8e-5245-4709-b433-c14b08365634.pdf

11
CROSSING DISCIPLINARY BOUNDARIES IN INCLUSIVE EDUCATION

Joanne Banks

Introduction

One of the unique aspects of the Inclusion Dialogue podcast is its informality. In engaging with often complex academic thinking, this format offers an alternative to traditional learning in its casual and unrehearsed format. The nature of dialogue itself is more than simple conversation, but suggests active listening, understanding, addressing tensions and challenging your assumptions. The chapters presented in this book seek to further strengthen these informal conversations by enabling the authors to expand on their ideas, detail their arguments and point readers to current research aligned with the various themes and research areas discussed. This chapter analyses the chapters included in this book and highlights some of the common themes, tensions and points of discussion raised.

The sociology of special education

Several of the contributors to Series 2 of the Inclusion Dialogue podcast and this book have sought, in their academic work, to bring the broader sociology of education perspectives into the special education literature. Powell's chapter describes the research challenge in connecting educational attainment and social stratification complicated further by variations in education structures across different national contexts and the persistence of special education structures. He situates the development of special education within the institutional design of education systems which stratify students through different school types, support structures and class compositions. Citing Tomlinson (2017) and his own work from 2014, he argues that:

> Where and when the general exclusion of pupils with impairments has been overcome through the development of special education programs, these

nevertheless frequently exhibit an overrepresentation of children living in poverty or in families with low socioeconomic status; boys and ethnic minorities (and children from migrant families from certain countries) are often considerably overrepresented.

Central to Powell's work on inclusive education is the need for comparative educational research to understand both the barriers to inclusion and how to overcome them and gain insights into inspiring inclusive educational practices. Detailing his involvement in an inclusive education comparative study (TdiverS project) with almost 20 partner countries he argues that:

cross-national collaborative projects promote in-depth comparison, cooperation, and understanding among representatives of countries with contrasting education systems and very different institutionalization pathways of inclusive schooling. Such exchange proves crucial in on-going inclusive education research and reform.

(Powell)

Tomlinson's chapter goes further and details the British history of social stratification and the role of disability and special education within this. She describes the system of the special and alternative education system in Britain as:

a mechanism for the social and economic control of the lower classes in the persistent British social class hierarchy.

(Tomlinson)

This chapter provides a history of special education from the 19th century within the context of social stratification and the beginning of the process of diagnosis of children by the medical profession with:

fears that a lower class of defective and disabled people would be an economic drain on society and become disruptive or criminal.

(Tomlinson)

Tomlinson's inclusion of this historical narrative is compelling as she forcefully aligns these historical processes with present-day systems of special education or 'deficit industry' which she believes is supported by:

expanded psychological and psychiatric and other professions claiming the ability to assess and treat what is now described as the neurodiversity of many of these children.

(Tomlinson)

Preparing our teachers and school leaders for inclusion

In her work in Asia, Forlin describes her academic work with colleagues seeking to measure changes in teacher attitudes to inclusion. She notes that over time, teacher attitudes have improved but highlight concerns such as 'unrealistic systemic expectations, crowded classrooms (especially across Asia & Africa), and their perceived inability to provide highly effective interventions and support for all learners' (Forlin). This point is picked up on by Powell also who argues that:

> teachers are often not aware of their true level of competences and inclusive practices developed in their everyday teaching.
>
> *(Powell)*

Sharma's chapter focuses firmly on the role of teacher education in inclusive education and provides a much-needed discussion on this crucial element in our education systems worldwide. Focusing on the 'Global South', he calls for the urgent reform of teacher education currently and simply poses the question '*is it possible that we have prepared teachers for exclusion and then we expect them to include all?*'. Sharma identifies five key principles to reform teacher education in the Global South but stresses that they can be applied to educational systems globally. He argues the need to build on the strengths of the current system acknowledging context, history and ancient and religious practices of inclusion and diversity. He describes how graduate teachers should work collaboratively with colleagues and emphasises the importance of simplifying the curriculum on inclusive education highlighting good teaching and understanding the learner rather than detailing various disabilities and running the risk of overwhelming student teachers.

Carrington opens her chapter with a call for critical reflection and action for those working in education. Her interview and chapter, however, focus firmly on inclusive school cultures and the importance of beliefs, values and practices in achieving meaningful inclusion. She highlights the critical role of school leaders in developing inclusive school cultures and nurturing relationships across the school community. She describes school leaders:

> transformational role that can impact individuals and the collective of staff, students, and parents in their school community by developing relationships that are equitable, caring, and open.

The role of school leadership is also referred to by Nairian who argues the need for learning diversity to be a foundational value of a school thus lessening the distinction between special and mainstream education. She links these values with how available funds are used in schools to the benefit of the school community and learner diversity. When this does not happen, she believes:

> the arrival of disabled students produces discourses of cost-benefit ratios rather than opportunities to enhance the quality of a community.
>
> *(Nairian)*

Critical junctures

Many of the authors detail their early career experiences offering insights into what has shaped their views on special and inclusive education today. A common thread underlies these conversations where, in their early careers, they were faced with systems of exclusion and segregation and 'social constructions of disability' (Carrington). In many cases, this acted as a catalyst for their life's work in seeking to understand, gather evidence and develop academic thinking around how to include every student regardless of their ability.

Working in India and the United States, Nairian describes how working with students with complex needs framed her present-day understanding of societal notions of capability or severity of disability. Again, she focuses on the role of parents in these early career experiences who, she noticed, had to:

> prove to school officials that their child could learn, grow and develop skills, even if they might look different from their grade-level peers.

This led Nairian to undertake ethnographic research in elementary classes where students with complex needs were included and she witnessed the use of 'elastic classroom structures' to facilitate inclusion.

Forlin describes her early career experiences of cultural diversity as critical in her understanding of inclusive education later in her academic work. On her first placements as a teacher, she describes large class sizes and little additional support at the school level and division among newly arrived immigrants to England and the local community. She believes there was little room for separation or segregation of any kind:

> As the new immigrants were not welcomed by the community, there was very much a divide between the two. In the very tight classrooms, though, there was no room for a divide, they were all mixed in together, and the children accepted it.
>
> *(Forlin)*

For Carrington, she witnessed a shift in the process of desegregation when a local special school in Cairns, Australia was closed and students moved to the mainstream school where she was working. She describes the parental advocacy that influenced the process of 'integration':

> All the students, teachers, nursing staff, therapists and teacher aides were transferred to local primary and secondary schools in Cairns to support a new process of education for students with disabilities.

However, these parents had a vision for inclusion and created momentum among school staff, challenging deficit views, reviewing practices and developing a collaborative and shared vision of inclusive education (Carrington).

Conceptual frameworks for understanding inclusion

Many of the chapters make reference to the value and importance of using theory and conceptual frameworks to help understand present-day educational policies and practices for children and young people. The social and medical models of disability offer a thread of understanding in several chapters as the way in which we frame conversations around special and inclusive education. This is perhaps best exemplified in Nairian's chapter which examines inclusion with a disability studies lens and seeks to understand the role of disability as analytic construct within education where ableist assumptions lead to labelling and categorisations of students as a way to explain variations in student ability and diversity more generally.

Given the depth of expertise among the authors in this book, many have considered ways in which the process of desegregation can work from a conceptual perspective. Carrington cites her recent work with her colleagues in QUT on diminishing the role of, and closing, special schools using research from Canada. In their conceptual framework, they highlight barriers to special school closure as operating at four levels: (1) societal level, (2) system level, (3) school level and (4) community level. This critical review is intended to inform policy decisions both in Australia and in countries internationally seeking to progress inclusive education systems.

Several authors describe the need for measurement and accountability in inclusive education and discuss the importance of measuring progress towards inclusion:

> how do schools know when they are getting better at inclusive education and that what they are doing is working?
>
> *(Forlin)*

In Sweden, Malmqvist also describes the need for great measurement of inclusion and inclusion and introduces an analytical tool for data collection known as the *Staircase Model of Inclusionary and Exclusionary Processes*. The model of assessment places emphasis on understanding both inclusionary and exclusionary forces both inside and outside the school to provide:

> researchers with a theoretical tool for more thoroughly understanding developments favouring inclusion versus exclusion in schools.
>
> *(Malmqvist)*

The inclusion plateau?

The book suggests that great changes are underway with regard to the implementation of inclusive education and highlight the progress made over the last three decades. However, several contributors expressed concern about the trajectory of inclusive education in different national contexts suggesting we are at risk of reaching an 'inclusion plateau'. In Sweden, Malmqvist highlights the 'weakening' of many of the country's inclusive policies in recent years and points to the increasing levels of diagnosis and special class placement for students with disabilities and in particular students with ADHD diagnosis:

> The large proportion of students receiving diagnoses, for example, of ADHD, reveals the popularity of medical explanations and treatments to address these issues…national policy of increasing the number of special education classes, pupil referral units (PRUs), and emergency schools (Ministry of Education, 2023), and thereby 'fixing' students' 'deficits' with exclusionary measures, seems to be the preferred way to address problems in the school system.
>
> *(Malmqvist)*

Powell also raises this as an issue in comparative research where he cites research in Germany and Nigeria which shows that 'segregated and separate settings have been maintained or even extended'. These trends are taking place in the context of the UNCRPD and Agenda 2030 and highlight either a reversal of inclusive policies or the beginning of segregated provision in some contexts. We are forced therefore to examine and re-examine what inclusive education is seeking to do. While the tide of opinion on the moral and legislative right to inclusive education dominates the discussion, there continue to be those who advocate for the maintenance, and perhaps more importantly, the improvement of our system of special education. Kauffman highlights the alternative perspective to the other contributors in this book and allows for reflection on the development of academic thinking around inclusion:

> I work within special education but against its poor practices or malpractice. My intent is improving special education. I do not work within it but against it with the intent of destroying it, undermining it, or delegitimizing it. I believe special education is a legitimate, necessary, and needed part of public education—and always will be.
>
> *(Kauffman)*

Kauffman challenges the clarity in the language used in the term 'all means all' and calls on academics and practitioners to '"come clean" linguistically' and say what they mean which is that there are always exceptions to inclusion for every child. He also raises the issue around the common comparison of disability as a barrier to education to other forms of diversity such as race as it is based on the assumption that:

> disabilities, like skin color, can be made irrelevant simply by removing legal and social barriers.
>
> *(Kauffman)*

Conclusion

These chapters bring together the lives, careers and outstanding academic contributions of critical academic thinkers in the field of special and inclusive education. This chapter provides an overview of the key points of tension raised in Series 2 of the Inclusion Dialogue podcast series and the subsequent chapters authored by the interviewees. Presenting a more holistic view of inclusion, the authors highlight the value of interdisciplinarity in understanding how education systems work within the context of historical, legal, moral, financial and social norms in countries around the world. The chapter details the wealth of scholarship available on the barriers to inclusion with a clear emphasis on 'process' rather than destination across many of the chapters. Within this process are the practical considerations in addressing issues of self-efficacy and capacity building among school leaders and teachers who are central to any inclusive ethos, culture and practice.

Reference

Tomlinson, S. (2017). *A sociology of special and inclusive education*. Routledge.

INDEX

Note: **Bold** indicates tables and *italics* indicates figures in the text. Page numbers followed by "n" refer to end notes.

additional learning need (ALN) 38
ADHD diagnosis 63, 126, 134
Ahsan, M. T. 3–4, 7–20
Ainscow, M. 28
'all means all' movement 47–48, 51, 53, 55, 135
Alternative Provision (AP) system 119, 126–127
Anastasiou, D. 50, 55
anti-classification 51–53
anti-special education 53–54
anti-subordination 51–53
Asadullah, N. 9
Asia 7–8, 35–37
Australian Professional Standards for Teachers 38
Australia, special schools in 24–30, 32–40, 42, 132–133

Badar, J. 48
Baglieri, S. 54
Bangladesh Bureau of Educational Information and Statistics (BANBEIS) 13
Bangladesh Bureau of Statistics (BBS) 13
Bangladesh Disability Welfare Act (2001) 10
Bangladesh, equity and inclusion in education: educational transformation 19–20; equity-related challenges 12–14; inclusion in education 11–12; National Curriculum 2022 15, **15–19**; policy on disability 9–10; pre-Bangladesh and Bangladesh period 8–9
Banks, J. 1–6, 23, 76–83, 86, 97, 109, 129–135
Bazna, M. S. 113
Berger, P. 124
Bradbury, M. 120
Burke, M. D. 54
Burt, C.: *The Young Delinquent* 122–123

Campaign for Popular Education (CAMPE) 13
Carrington, S. 4, 23–30, 131–133
Centre for Social Justice 125
Chronically Sick and Disabled Persons Act (1970) 126
Cline, T. 125
Cole, T. 69
Compulsory Primary Education Act (1990) 9
Connor, D. J. 54
continuum of alternative placements (CAP) 52, 55
Cook, I. 2–3
Covid-19 pandemic 14, 38–40, 127
critical thinking 24

cross-national collaborative projects 106, 130
cultural diversity 32–33, 132

Daniels, H. 69
decision-making 38, 42, 71, 93, 100
deep exclusion 68–69
defective children 120–122, 124–125, 130
disability 7–11, 25–29, 38–42, 51–58, 76–84, 90, 93, 96–102, 110–111, 113–114, 130–135; inclusion/inclusive education 86–89; intellectual 51, 78; neuropsychiatric 71, 73n6; policy on 9–10
disability studies in education (DSE) 46, 51, 54
discrimination 47–49, 52, 72, 97–98, 100
diversity 1, 3, 5, 8, 32–33, 39–42, 48, 51–54, 57, 86, 89, 98, 101, 104, 106, 110, 112, 131–133, 135
diversity, equity, and inclusion (DEI) 52
Dunn, L. M. 51

Education Act (2014) 126
educationally subnormal (ESN) schools 120 121, 123–124
educational realities 56–58
Education for All Children Act 50
Education for All Handicapped Children Act of 1975 (EAHCA) 45–46, 52–54
Education, Health and Care Plans (EHCP) 126
Education University of Hong Kong (EDUHK) 35
England 26, 32–35, 72, 119, 124–126, 132
European Agency for Special Needs and Inclusive Education (EASIE) 72, 102
Europe, special and inclusive education 96–97; comparative analysis 101; effect 105–106; implementation 104–105; institutional design and factors 100–101; life course 97–98; multidisciplinary field 98–100; SEN classification rates 101–103; sustainability 104

Forlin, C. 4, 32–42, 131–132
Frederickson, N. 125
Free special schools 126
Fuchs, D. 54, 58
Fuchs, L. S. 54, 58
full inclusion movement (FIM) 54–55, 58

Gabel, S. 4, 76–84
Giangreco, M. F. 24
Global North 2, 6, 86, 90–91
Global South 2, 6, 86, 90, 113, 131
Göransson, K. 68
graduate teachers 111–112, 114–115, 131
Greenhouse, L. 47–48
Gren Landell, M. 63
Gulliford, R., *Special Educational Needs* 120
Gurukul system 113

habeas corpus 48, 56
Hallahan, D. P. 54
handicapped children 68, 120, 123
Harden, K. P. 51
Hatab, T. A. 113
Head of Special Education 27
Hedegaard Hansen, J. 68
Hernshaw, L. 122
Hong Kong schools 35–37

inclusion/inclusive education 11–12, 24–28, 86; colonial approach to 111–112; dilemmas of practice 89–91; misconception 111; North and South conceptions 90; teachers and school leaders for 131–132; teaching practice 91–93; through disability 86–89
Inclusive Research on Equity and Segregation in Schools (IRESS) 64
inclusive schools 1, 4, 6, 27–29, 87, 90–91, 104, 106, 110, 112, 117, 130–131
India 8, 87, 89, 110, 113, 132
Individual Education Programmes (IEPs) 27
Individuals with Disabilities Education Improvement Act (IDEA) 45–46, 52–54, 84, 97
inside school forces 69
integration process 26
intellectual disability (ID) 51, 78
Intellectual Property Statistical Country Profile 2022 Index 13
intersectional special education 78–80

January Agreement 63, 73n2
judgment-making 49

Kaplan, I. 12
Kauffman, J. M. 4–5, 45–58, 134–135
Krauss, L. A. 55, 57
Kudrat-E-Khuda Education Commission 9

Laski, F. J. 55
least restrictive environment (LRE) 52
Lewis, I. 12
life course approach 97–99
line-drawing 49–51

Malak, M. S. 8
Malmqvist, J. 5, 62–73, 133–134
Mattingly, J. 12
McQueen, Steve 120
McRuer, R. 93n1
mental: defectives 121; health issues 39; illness 51; retardation 51; testing movement 122
middle-class interests 125–126
Miles, M. 113
Miller, A. 4, 76–84
Ministry of Education (MoE) 14
Mitchell, G. 124
multiacademy trusts (MATS) 126
multi-tiered system of supports (MTSS) 54
Myklebust, J. O. 69
myths and delusions 51

Naraian, S. 5, 86–93
National Consistent Collection of Data (NCCD) 38
National Curriculum and Textbook Board (NCTB) 14
National Curriculum Framework-2021 (NCF) 14–15
National Education Policy (NEP) 2010 9
National Policy for the Disabled 10
National School Commission 63
National Student Assessment (NSA) 13
Nes, K. 69
neurodiversity 125–126, 130
neuropsychiatric disabilities 71, 73n6
new public management (NPM) 62, 72
Nilholm, C. 64, 68

Oliver, M. 54
Oppositional Conduct Disorder (OCD) 126
Orwell, G. 47
outside school forces 70

Pakistan 8–9, 113
Parents' Perceptions of Home-schooling (PPHS) scale 40
placement 25, 39, 41, 47, 51–52, 54–55, 63, 67, 73n1, 89, 92, 102, 106, 110, 112, 122–123, 126–127, 132, 134

Powell, J. J. W., *Living at the Heart of the UVA Community* 5, 96–106, 129–131, 134
pre-service teachers 37, 115–116
Primary Education Development Programme Phase 2 (PEDP II) 10–12
problem solving 51–53
Project IRIS 70
proprium instructio inclusion 48
pupil referral units (PRUs) 63, 67, 70, 124, 126, 134
push–pull factor theory 69–70

Queensland University of Technology (QUT) 24–26, 28, 34–35
Quranic analysis 114

regular schools 24–27, 33–36, 39, 65–67, 78, 110–111
Reynold, M. D. 68
Rights and Protection of Persons with Disabilities Act, 2013 10
Robbins, A. 57

Safety Valve programme 122
Sailor, W. 55
Salamanca Declaration 7, 101
School Commission 70
Scotland 124
Selective Service Act 45
self-stimulation 26
Shannon, L. 120
Sharma, U. 5–6, 109–117, 131
Shields, C. 23, 29
significantly disabled 86–88, 90, 93n1
Singh, R. 113
Slee, R. 25, 54
social class 120–122
sociology of special education 129–130
Southard School 45
special educational needs (SEN) 97–102, 105
special educational needs and disabilities (SEND) 48–58, 119, 122, 125–127
special education units (SEUs) 28
Special needs and Alternative Provision Improvement Plan 126
special schools: in Australia 24–30; barriers to 133; free 126
Staircase Model of Inclusionary and Exclusionary Processes 62, 64, *65*, 73, 133–134
students with disabilities (SWD) 48
Sustainable Development Goals (SDGs) 64, 98, 101, 106

Sweden 63–65, 67–68, 71–72, 73n3, 102–103, 133–134
Swedish National Agency for Education 71
Swedish National Board of Institutional Care (SiS) 67
Swedish schools 71–73; dynamics 68–69; exclusionary development trajectory 62–64; inside school forces 69; outside school forces 70; societal mechanisms 70; staircase model 64–68, *65*; transactional theory 71

Taylor, J. L. 55
Taylor, S. J. 55
TdiverS Project 102–103, 106, 130
teacher education systems, principles 111–113, 116–117; building upon strengths 113–114; collective collaboration 114, inclusion as a norm 115; simplicity in approach 114–115; student and parent/carer voices 115–116
Teaching Quality Improvement (TQI) project 11–12
Tomlinson, S. 6, 119–127, 129–130
transactional theory 71
transformative school leadership 29
Tredgold, R., *Mental Deficiency* 121

uncertainty 49–51
UN Convention on the Right of Persons with Disability (UN CRPD) 7, 97–98, 101–104
United Nations Convention on the Rights of Persons with Disabilities (UNCRPD) 82, 89, 134
United States 46, 83–84, 97, 106, 132; career experiences 76–77; language complexity and change over time 77–78; legislation and accountability 80–81; special education research 78–80; teacher education, policy influences on 81–83
Universal Design for Learning (UDL) 15
U.S. law 55

vernacularization 91
Volatile, Uncertain, Complex, Ambiguous (VUCA) 38–40

Walker, H. M. 46
Warnock, M. 49, 120, 123
Whelan, R. J. (Dick) 45
word meanings 47–50

Zambia schools 35

For Product Safety Concerns and Information please contact our EU representative GPSR@taylorandfrancis.com Taylor & Francis Verlag GmbH, Kaufingerstraße 24, 80331 München, Germany